The

ORGANIC
GOD

FALL IN LOVE WITH GOD ALL OVER AGAIN

Since the first printing of this book, something, well, rather organic has been happening. Readers have been making little handwritten notes in the front of the book of things they've learned about God, then passing the book along to someone else. So we figured that we'd invite you to join the conversation. And while you're at it, we'd love to know: What do you love about Jesus?

_____

_____

_____

_____

_____

_____

_____

_____

_____

_____

_____

_____

_____

_____

_____

_____

The ORGANIC GOD

Fall in Love with God All Over Again

MARGARET FEINBERG

ZONDERVAN®

ZONDERVAN.com/
AUTHORTRACKER
follow your favorite authors

ZONDERVAN

The Organic God
Copyright © 2007 by Margaret Feinberg

Requests for information should be addressed to:

Zondervan, *Grand Rapids, Michigan 49530*

ISBN 978-0-310-32986-2

Published in association with Christopher Ferebee.com, Attorney and Literary Agent.

Cover design: Curt Diepenhorst
Cover photography: Shutterstock®
Interior design: Beth Shagene with Sarah Johnson

Printed in the United States of America

13 14 15 16 17 18 /DCI/ 21 20 19 18 17 16 15 14 13 12 11 10 9 8 7 6 5 4 3 2

Contents

.000 Luminescence

THE NORTHERN LIGHTS DANCED WITH ALL THE MYSTERY
and marvel of midnight rainbows in the sky. Under star-
filled heavens, Kacy and her husband Toby were enjoying
a much-needed getaway on their thirty-four-foot, baby blue
Tollycraft anchored near Auke Bay, Alaska. Sitting on the
deck of their boat, Kacy looked into the sea and began to
notice tiny, mysterious sparkles of luminescence. This magical
light is known as bioluminescence, a process in which marine
organisms produce light as a result of a chemical reaction
involving the oxidation of a substrate molecule luciferin by
a catalyst luciferase; the energy is released as sparkling blue-
green light.

Like many of us who respond to natural wonders, Kacy wasn't
interested in a science lesson. She didn't even care what the
mysterious sparkles were called. She was too caught up in the
beauty of the moment.

Kacy grabbed a broom handle resting in the corner of the boat,
stirred up the water, and watched with glee as the sea came to

life in all its secret shimmering beauty. "How could you not have told me?" she asked her husband with a blend of contempt and disbelief. Raised in Michigan, she had been living in the waterfront town of Juneau, Alaska, for more than four years and had missed experiencing this luminous wonder until now.

A week after the getaway, Kacy was still in awe of her find. As she recounted the story, she asked me, "Did you know? Have you heard?" I smiled, recalling the excitement I felt as a child during my first encounter with luminescence. I shared that unforgettable moment with my mom as she gently explained that these fireflies of the sea were actually living creatures. At that moment, something in me came alive that I can't quite explain. Years later, I still carry the same sense of childlike wonder whenever I think about luminescence.

Whenever I encounter something new that represents everything that is good and true and beautiful, something awakens inside of me. Maybe it's a heart cry for the Creator or maybe it's the Creator's heart cry for me. I do not know, but such encounters remind me that there is so much more to do and experience and know—not just about my world but about my God.

This book is designed to take you on a journey and to illuminate the beauty of God in your life. It asks you to open your eyes to some of the things God has been doing all along that you may have missed or that no one has ever told you about. My hope and prayer is that through this book you'll fall in love with God again for the first time, and that a part of you will come alive as you dance in all the brilliance of his design.

Blessings,
Margaret

.001 An Organic Appetite

It was one thing for my Jewish father to marry my non-Jewish mother, but another thing completely for both of them to become Christians within a month of each other eight years into their marriage. Let's just say that the decision did not go down too well with the Jewish side of the family. (Imagine *My Big Fat Greek Wedding* without the happy ending.) A month after their conversion, I was conceived, and less than a year later, I was welcomed into a world of religious tension. I didn't know it at the time, but I became the bundle of glue that held the family together, because as upset as my Jewish grandmother was at my father, she wasn't going to give up access to her only grandchild.

As a result of my parents' backgrounds, I was raised in a Christian home with hues of Judaism. Think matza ball soup at Christmastime. I never knew how many gifts my Jewish grandmother was going to give—whether I would hit the jackpot with the stack-o-gifts that accompanies Hanukkah, or receive the one big present that inadvertently acknowledged Christmas even though it was still wrapped in Hanukkah paper. The confusion ended when Grandma began giving the gift that embraced the fullness of my Jewish heritage: a check.

Throughout the years, I managed to learn a few random Yiddish words, develop a quirky Jewish sense of humor, and inherit an undeniable sense of chutzpah. I developed a desire to know how these worlds that seemed so opposed in my childhood could ever get along. I also developed a hunger to know God. This hunger wasn't anything I conjured up but rather seemed to be part of the "me-package," like a strand of DNA, though it took years to fully manifest itself. My initial interaction with Scripture wasn't born out of longing as much as desperation. I was having terrible nightmares — the kind you can't forget even when you're an adult.

On a sunny, breeze-softened afternoon, I was fishing alongside a creek in a forest filled with maple and oak trees. Sitting on the moss-carpeted shore, I held a thin wooden fishing pole. I felt a slight tug on the line and an unmistakable surge of excitement. I began pulling back on the pole which arched at the weight of the catch. Without warning, a huge shark with beady eyes and enormous yellow razor-sharp teeth came out of the water and toward my face.

I awoke, breathless. Heart pounding. Body covered in sweat. I knew sharks didn't jump out of creeks and eat people, but now I wasn't so sure. I didn't want to fall back asleep ever again. Would the next nightmare be worse?

The night terrors continued for months. My parents held me. Prayed for me. Comforted me when they heard my screams.

But the dreams didn't stop until I made a personal discovery. Somehow, I figured out that if I read the Bible before I went to bed, I would sleep soundly. It's a strange equation:

Bible before bed = No nightmares

The concept made perfect sense when I was eight. I couldn't explain why it worked, I just knew that it did. And when you're facing man-eating sharks, you'll do whatever it takes to make them go away.

Two-plus decades later, I'm sometimes tempted to shrug off my miracle cure as an oddity or merely chance, except for the fact that those evening readings made God all the more real and personal. I'm humbled that God would so tenderly and intimately embrace a child with simple faith. And I am staggered to realize how God was preparing me, even then, to know him better.

Somewhere along the way, reading the Bible became enjoyable and not just a cure for nightmares. The stories of kings and queens and prophets and pilgrims came alive, and of course, the Jesus-man captured my heart as well as my imagination. What did he look like? What did his voice sound like? What did his hands feel like? I wanted to know.

Now there were a few years when I forgot about my experience as a young girl. I tried to run away from God and engaged in an extracurricular activity better known as partying like a rock star. I kissed too many boys and drank too much beer and enjoyed a thoroughly hollow good time, but deep down inside, I knew that partying wasn't the life for me. I returned to the routine I had learned at eight years old and began reading my Bible again.

More than a decade later, I still want to know God. The desire hasn't cooled. At times I have allowed myself to be overpowered by other desires. Busyness. Lesser loves. Laziness. And the temptation to let someone else do the hard work of digging into the rich reservoirs of Scripture.

All too often I find myself tempted to live a distracted life. You know the kind — the one where, within the busyness of life, you still manage to perform the stand-up, sit-down, clap, clap, clap of regular church attendance; drop a check in the offering plate; hope for a new nugget of knowledge, understanding, or insight in the weekly sermon; and check off a random, albeit short, list of acts of kindness to others. Somehow I'm supposed to feel like I'm living the Jesus-driven life.

I don't.

That's when the hunger appears in my belly and overtakes my soul, grumbling that there must be more. Even in the mundane, I find myself wanting more of God. Surely I'm not the only person who lies in bed at night wondering, *Is this all there is?* I can't be the only one who looks at the seemingly rich buffet of everything this world has to offer and loses my appetite, because even with countless provisions, friends, and activities — many of which are not only good but could be classified as godly — I can't shake this sense that there's more.

The hunger growls that there's more of God not only to uncover but to discover.

The hunger cries out that there's more of this God-infused life to live.

The hunger reminds me that there's more.

I want to go there. But how do I find the way?

When I reflect on my life map so far, I realize that spiritual hunger, the enablement to love and long for a relationship with our Creator, is both God's greatest command and his greatest gift. It's the kind of desire that compelled the psalmist not only to ask, "Whom have I in heaven but you?" but to answer, "Earth has nothing I desire besides you."

That's why I began praying for spiritual hunger and haven't stopped. As my prayers funnel toward heaven, I can't help but reflect on my own spiritual journey and wonder how much of God I really know and how much of God I simply take other people's word for or dismiss altogether. If God is bighearted, then why am I tempted to live with a closed hand? If God is surprisingly talkative, then why don't I take more time to listen? If God is deeply mysterious, then why do I sometimes lose the intrigue?

In the quietness of my own soul, I cannot help but wonder, *How much of God do I really know?*

If we met on the street, would I even recognize him?

In the humility of honesty and a soul laid bare: I do not know.

Such realizations shake the core of who I am. I'm pointedly reminded of the day an older woman I barely knew asked if my mother was Jewish when she heard my last name.

"No, just my father," I explained.

"Well, then you're not Jewish," she replied. "To be Jewish, your mom must be Jewish."

I was taken aback. I had a Jewish father, a Jewish grandmother who escaped Poland at the onset of World War II, and I knew how to make a mean bowl of matza ball soup. Even my best friend was Jewish. What more did you have to do to be a half-Jew?

It turned out that nosy woman was right. Orthodox Judaism embraces matrilineal descent, or the belief that a child's Jewish identity is passed down through the mother. Only recently has the reformed movement within Judaism embraced patrilineal descent. Regardless, they still require that the child be raised Jewish—which I was not.

The incident left me feeling like a spiritual bastard child. Once the paralyzing effect of the conversation wore off and my mom assured me that I was my father's daughter, I grew an even deeper desire to understand how these two worlds—that of Jewish descent and Christian upbringing—intersect. It also left me hungrier for God. What does it mean to be his child? How does that affect my identity, my behavior, the very core of who I am? I knew he was the only one who could offer any resolve.

Deep down inside I still hunger for a true, pure relationship with the Organic God—the One True God. The God of Abraham, Isaac, and Jacob. In him is found the mysterious wonder of the Trinity. He is Father, Son, and Holy Spirit— one luminous essence in whom there is no shadow of change, stirred by the eternal and dynamic relationship of the three persons who live and love completely free of any need or self-interest.

Why describe God as organic? More and more I realize that my own understanding of God is largely polluted. I have preconceived notions, thoughts, and biases when it comes to God. I have a tendency to favor certain portions of Scripture over others. I have a bad habit of reading some stories with a been-there-done-that attitude, knowing the end of the story before it begins, and in the process denying God's ability to speak to me through it once again.

If that weren't enough, more often than not, I find myself compartmentalizing God. He is more welcome in some areas of my life than others. Prayer, Bible study, Scripture memorization, journaling, and other spiritual disciplines become like items to be checked off a to-do list that is eventually crumpled up and thrown away rather than savored and reflected upon. The result is that my understanding and perception of God is clouded, much like the dingy haze of pollution that hangs over most major cities. The person in the middle of a city looking up at the sky doesn't always realize just how much their view and perceptions are altered by the smog. Without symptoms such as burning eyes or an official warning of scientists or media, no one may even notice just how bad the pollution has become.

That's why I describe God as organic. While it's a word usually associated with food grown without chemical-based fertilizers or pesticides, *organic* is also used to describe a lifestyle: simple, healthful, and close to nature. Those are all things I desire in my relationship with God. I hunger for the simplicity. I want to approach God in childlike faith, wonder, and awe. I long for more than just spiritual life but spiritual health — whereby my soul is not just renewed and restored but becomes a source of refreshment for others. And I want to be close to nature, not mountain ridges and shorelines as much as God's nature working in and through me. Such a God-infused lifestyle requires me to step away from any insta-grow shortcuts and dig deep into the soil of spiritual formation found only in God.

Natural. Pure. Essential.

I want to discover God again, anew, in a fresh way. I want my love for him to come alive again so that my heart dances at the very thought of him. I want a real relationship with him—a relationship that isn't altered by perfumes, additives, chemicals, or artificial flavors that promise to make it sweeter, sourer, or tastier than it really is. I want to know a God who in all his fullness would allow me to know him. I want a relationship that is real, authentic, and life-giving even when it hurts. I want to know God stripped of as many false perceptions as possible. Such a journey risks exposure, honesty, and even pain, but I'm hungry and desperate enough to go there.

I want to know the Organic God.

I have this hunch that when God grants us a whim or a whiff of a desire to know him, we should take action—and fast —because those windows of opportunity may pass, and we may once again become satisfied with the smorgasbord of this world, rather than the world to come. I knew I had to do something, but what?

I decided once again to read the book that God gave me.

You probably have a copy too. Usually when I give a book to someone, I want to build a relationship — to develop conversation, share ideas, and grow together. The gift of a book is a tangible effort to take the relationship to a new intensity — so it becomes deeper, richer, and broader than ever before.

Recognizing that you cannot love that which you do not know and experience, I began my journey to know God more by going through key books of the Old Testament and the entire New Testament, recording every verse that described a characteristic or attribute of God. As you can imagine, I've filled dozens and dozens of pages. Along the way, I found unimaginably breathtaking aspects of God.

In some regards, the journey to know God isn't too different from a first encounter with someone you've never met. I want to know what God looks like and what his interests are. I want to know his likes and dislikes. I want to know what makes him tick and also what ticks him off. I want to fall in love all over again. I want to know God.

Through the Scripture, God invites us to discover the wonders of Jesus shining in its pages. But it takes work. Like peeling an orange, reading the Bible sometimes feels messy and sticky and time-consuming. But once you bite into its pulpy juiciness — oh, how its flavors dance on the taste buds.

And while we relish the taste, the nutrients also feed our soul.

With the Spirit's enzymes, we unknowingly, automatically, miraculously digest the words on the page, until they transform our actions and even our attitudes. Indeed, the book God gives us is like no other. God seems far more concerned with transformation than mere information. If you look real close, you'll notice that scrawled on every page is an invitation to know the author.

God glows. His glory illuminates the heavens. Jesus, by his very nature, is brilliance. The One described as the light of the world does not contain a shadow of darkness. And the Holy Spirit ushers the spiritual dawn into our lives. Like the fireflies of the sea that beckon our imaginations to another world, the truth of God invites us to embrace the fullness of the life we were meant to live. As we look to him, we can't help but become more radiant.

The vastness. The beauty. The power. The splendor. The glory.

It looks like luminescence is already beginning to surface.

.002 Bighearted

I LIVED IN SO MANY DIFFERENT PLACES GROWING UP THAT
people used to ask me if my dad was in the military. He wasn't.
Neither was my mom. Rather, they were both adventurers.
I'd use the word *free-spirited*, but that term has a connotation
of the sixties free-love movement, hippie-length hair, and
Volkswagen vans.

My parents drove a Volvo.

While in his early twenties, my dad began manufacturing
surfboards on the East Coast. It was a highly successful
business until he lost everything (and more) through a series of
fires. Around the same time, he met my mom, who was young,
blonde, and looking for a discount on a surfboard. They fell
in love. Dad waited until after Mom said *I do* to reveal that he
wasn't just broke, he was drowning in debt.

She stuck around anyway.

My parents quit manufacturing surfboards and started selling
them directly instead. They managed to climb out of debt and
open Oceanside Surf Shop in Cocoa Beach, Florida, on A1A.
I grew up around racks of surfboards, stacks of Levi jeans, and

too many bathing suits to count. I can still smell Mr. Zog's surfboard wax when I think about it now.

Neither Mom nor Dad is good at sitting still. When I was the ripe young age of two, my parents were having dinner at a restaurant on the water, watching the boats go by, when on a whim, they thought it would be fun to start sailing. Within a week, they called a yacht broker and purchased a small boat. Though they knew nothing about operating a boat, let alone a sailboat, they decided to make the hundred-plus-mile journey to the Bahamas.

They quickly enrolled me in swimming lessons in case I fell overboard.

Within a few months, we were on the adventure of a lifetime, complete with breathtaking sunsets, lobster dinners, and wildly colorful underwater reefs. The trip also included mechanical problems, unexpected storms, and running aground. Despite the difficulties, we all felt alive on the boat, and sailing became a regular part of our family life.

We returned to the Bahamas many times throughout the years. Instead of attending third grade, I spent most of the school year living on the boat with my parents. Mom was brave enough to enroll me in a homeschool program long before homeschooling was considered a reputable form of education. I quickly figured out that if I did all my work on one day of the week, I could be free to swim, dive, and explore on the other six. Maybe the education wasn't that reputable after all, but regardless, it was a wildly adventurous year.

When we finally sailed into our home port in Florida, my parents had lost all interest in the surf shop. They decided to sell their business and home and move to the mountains.

We packed up a U-Haul and made the trek to Maggie Valley, North Carolina, a town that my mom had visited as a child. I was only eight. It was the early 1980s and the move came at a rather tense time during the Cold War, so my parents decided our property should include a natural well, a bomb shelter, and a box garden. We were a completely self-sufficient homestead just in case World War III suddenly erupted.

Ten years later we were still trying to sell off survival supplies. I look back on those years and wonder, *What were they thinking?* If I had to choose between a nuclear bomb or living on canned tofu and lima beans post-contamination, I'd opt for the nuke any day.

While preparing for the end of the world was entertaining, it wasn't exactly a source of income, so Mom took a job teaching elementary school on the Cherokee Indian reservation, and Dad worked on construction projects. During the winters, Mom worked as a ski instructor and Dad as a ski patrol at the local ski area. I became a master sledder on the hill behind our home. During the summers, we hiked the Blue Ridge Mountains and picked the world's sweetest wild strawberries.

I remember one summer my parents decided to plant an acre of Silver Queen corn. Corn wasn't exactly an upgrade to our end-of-the-world diet plan, but I also knew it could have been worse. We could have planted brussels sprouts.

My parents were excited about growing their own food, so excited, in fact, that they never calculated just how much corn you can grow on an acre.

One hot summer day we drove down a dusty gravel road to our acre of Silver Queen corn. Mom decided to stake her claim by pulling off a ripe ear, peeling back the green husk, and biting into its raw, fresh sweetness. She handed the ear to my dad, who took a bite before passing it on to me. The corn tasted more like sugar than any vegetable I had ever eaten. Maybe the end of the world wasn't going to be so bad after all.

We spent the next few hours picking corn and barely cleared a single row. I plucked the ears closer to the base of the stalk, which were within reach, while my parents harvested the higher ones. Like ants, we carried the corn back to the truck in an organized fashion. At some point, my dad came to his senses and said, "That's enough."

We crammed into the truck all hot and sticky with sweat, slightly dehydrated, and nauseous from eating so much raw corn. Looking back, I wish I had known more about child labor laws. While my parents had given some thought to planting and harvesting the corn, they had never really considered what they would do with all that corn, or worse, who would prepare all that corn for whatever they decided to do with it.

Late into the evening, we sat on the front porch shucking corn. Meanwhile, Mom was having a full Forrest Gump epiphany: "We could have frozen corn and canned corn and cream of corn and corn chowder and maybe we could make corn syrup and popcorn." *What did fried corn taste like?* I didn't want to know.

By the end of the summer, we had cleared less than five rows of stalks in our acre, but our bomb shelter was fully loaded with all kinds of corn concoctions. I am embarrassed to admit that we donated some of them to charity.

God forgive us.

The Appalachian chapter of our journey lasted for less than five years. As usual, Mom and Dad got the itch to try something new. After too many winters skiing sheets of ice in western North Carolina, they decided to pack up and spend a winter working at a ski area in Colorado. My parents pulled me out of school again, packed up a mountain of ski gear and the family dog, and drove to Denver, Colorado, where we took a family vote about whether to spend the ski season in Aspen or Steamboat Springs, Colorado. The votes were unanimous —we were on our way to Steamboat.

I loved the winter in Colorado, my new friends, and the winter fun. When the snow began to melt, I asked Mom and Dad if we could stay. They thought it was a great idea, and we made our home in Steamboat for the next fourteen years. To this day, I still consider Colorado home.

Today, my parents have come full circle in their life: they live in a cottage they built for themselves in the Bahamas. Meanwhile, I live in Alaska. Our locations and lives are very different, but in many ways they are very much the same. Both pluses and minuses accompany an adventure-driven life. In some regards, living in so many places was difficult. I would begin to make close friends in one town or port, and then be pulled away to another. I remember when we moved to North Carolina in fourth grade, everyone knew how to play kickball except me. I could name dozens of different fish and types of coral, but simple elementary school games proved difficult and sometimes silly. At the same time, the years of travel and moving exposed me to so many different people, places, and experiences, I can't help but think I was enriched by the journey.

One of the things that I appreciate most as I reflect on this nontraditional upbringing is that wherever we lived or traveled, my parents, and especially my dad, were always connecting with people. Whether he was on a ski slope or a dive boat, Dad was constantly listening, learning, and exchanging ideas and stories. While he sometimes dreaded going to social events, he was usually the one we had to drag away at the end of the night.

Once my dad made a personal connection with someone, he would do anything for them. When he owned a surf shop, he was constantly helping out single moms and those in need by giving them free clothes. When we lived on the boat, he would help those on the dock fix everything from their engine to their toilet. When we lived in western Colorado, he helped build fences and shovel manure on a friend's ranch. He wasn't above getting down in the dirt of people's lives and making a difference.

In a word, my dad is bighearted.

He simply loved to be with people. For my dad, the simplest request for help was an opportunity for relationship. It wasn't about the act of service as much as it was an expression of love, care, and companionship.

I not only saw this in his relationships with others, I experienced it in my interactions with him. My father was always gracing me with more than I deserved or even asked for. One of the best portraits of this came when I needed to ask my father for money. I was always a bit shy about making the request, but I would eventually work up the courage to let my dad know my need. The conversation usually went something like this, "Dad, can I have some money for the movies this weekend?" To which my dad would always ask, "Well, how much do you need?"

For whatever reason, I would ask for a low amount. I don't know if my dad ever knew that I would secretly hold back my true need, but it didn't matter because he would always give me more than I asked for. It never failed. If I asked for ten dollars, he would give me twenty. If I asked for twenty, he would give me thirty or forty. My dad never gave me what I requested; he always gave me more.

In the process, he gave me something else: an incredibly graceful understanding of how our heavenly Father interacts with us. Just like my dad, God is very bighearted. In every circumstance, he doesn't just give us what we ask for, or even what we need. He gives us more, and in the process, invites us into a deeper relationship with him. He gives us those things we can't even identify or put into words. He lavishes us with his love and care. He doesn't hold back from the grit and grime of our lives. He gives of himself. He interacts with us in ways we didn't think possible. He speaks to us, he listens to us, he sings to us — he even dances over us. Indeed, our God is very bighearted.

Why reflect on God's bigheartedness? Psalm 107:43 puts it succinctly: "Whoever is wise, let him heed these things and consider the great love of the LORD."

When we talk about a bighearted God, we find a God whose love cannot be contained, coupled by desire for real relationship. It's immeasurable. It's so big that in Ephesians 3:17–19, Paul offers up this prayer:

> And I pray that you, being rooted and established in love, may have power, together with all the saints, to grasp how wide and long and high and deep is the love of Christ, and to know this love that surpasses knowledge — that you may be filled to the measure of all the fullness of God.

The length, height, and depth express the incomprehensible size and the unimaginable recesses of God's love. His love reaches beyond what we can fathom. He permeates creation with his glory. Some theologians even suggest that such a perfect cube — in length, height, and depth — is reflective of the Holy of Holies. No matter how you read these verses, a portrait of God's bighearted love and his desire for relationship emerges.

Such divine words are not simply mantras to be memorized. They come alive in our interactions with God. In his bigheartedness, God is not above putting his love on display in our lives in intimate, personal ways, yet the greatest portraits of

God's love are not found in personal experiences but in his Son as revealed in Scripture.

In Jesus, God put his whole heart on display for the world to see. In Jesus, my love for God is renewed. In Jesus, the fullness of God's bigheartedness is revealed. I don't know what it is about him, but something about Jesus steadies me. His words breathe life. His actions impart hope. His life inspires action. It's not just his selflessness — that he would die for the redemption of others. The very act of coming to this world as one of us — the incarnational element of Christ — is so revealing, so compelling. Jesus gave up the comforts, pleasures, and beauty of heaven to be reduced to human form in a rundown stable in a less than popular area of town. He was literally born into the stench of this world, and he embraced those in it. He went after the untouchable, the unapproachable, and the questionable.

This incarnational element, the kind where Jesus becomes one of us, was wonderfully demonstrated in *Motorcycle Diaries*. The film follows Ernesto Guevara, played by Gael García Bernal, and Alberto Granado, played by Rodrigo de la Serna, on a 1950s motorcycle trip across South America. The movie focuses on the tragedies and triumphs of their journey, the people they encounter, and a rich mixture of ironies as well as injustices.

A slow documentary, the film barely keeps you holding on for the next scene. I watched it after being in airports all day and found myself dozing in and out of sleep and various scenes, but one part of the movie gripped my heart.

Toward the end of the film, the motorcycle duo spent time offering medical help to a lepers' colony. The nuns who cared for the lepers required that everyone wear gloves for fear of being infected. Sadly, the gloves represented the way those with leprosy are treated — professionally, and at a distance. Ernesto refuses the gloves. With his bare hands, he touches those with leprosy. He talks to them as people. He laughs. He embraces. In the process, he comes fully alive and spreads that contagious life to everyone he meets. The film is one of the best portrayals I have ever seen of choosing to live incarnationally.

What does it look like to enter into someone's life? To embrace without hesitance? To be fully human?

It looks like the person of Jesus.

Now there were a lot of days growing up that I didn't look anything like Jesus. In fact, there were more than a handful of days during my childhood when I was more like the anti-Jesus in my behavior, actions, or attitudes than any other kid. Need proof? Just ask my mom.

Like most kids, I also had a handful of good moments — those God-infused times that I can still look back and smile on. I remember one school year when the mean kids were really getting to me. They weren't bothering me personally, but I remember standing by silently and watching two seventh-grade girls get picked on unmercifully. I couldn't figure out why. Now it didn't help that one of the girl's last names rhymed with *nasty*, but other than that unavoidable and rather unlucky junior high faux paux, there was no reason to taunt them (as if there ever is). Yet the bullies verbally tore the girls to pieces. Other kids wouldn't talk to them for fear of the same treatment. At lunch, they were guaranteed their own table, because no one dared sit by them. I was new to the school but made friends quickly. Across the lunchroom, I watched the two girls, who were obviously best friends, eat their lunches—as well as watched the verbal haranguing and social ostracizing they endured. I thought, *What if that was me?* For weeks I watched from a safe distance, and with each bullying incident, I grew more and more angry. I knew what the kids were doing was wrong, but I didn't know how to fix the situation. One day, I made a conscious decision to try to change things. I picked up my lunchroom tray and made a beeline for their table. I introduced myself and asked if I could sit with them. They looked at me, surprised.

You don't want to sit with us, one of the girls said hesitantly.

Yes, I do.

I could feel the eyes of the other kids in the lunchroom on me

35

—but I didn't care. Looking back, I think that was one of the scariest, yet most liberating moments of my childhood. I had made an active decision, an incarnational effort, to enter someone else's world. I sat at their table every day from then on. We became friends—complete with slumber parties, shared snacks, and all the awkwardness that accompanies being in junior high. Several well-meaning classmates pulled me aside and warned me that I was making a bad decision, but it's one that I've never regretted.

Not long after, some of the kids began targeting some of their comments and aggression toward me when I was hanging with the two gals, but somehow, knowing that you're enduring some sort of hardship because you care about someone else makes it hurt just a little bit less. And I lucked out that not a whole lot rhymes with "Feinberg."

Less than two months later, my parents announced that we were going to spend the winter in Colorado. I said goodbye to my two friends, my only two *real* friends at the time, and headed West with my family. Even as a seventh grader, I had this sense that to become part of someone's life, even when it wasn't the most popular decision, was something that Jesus would have done.

Staring at the various scenes in Jesus's life, we are exposed to his enormous heart for us. One of my favorites is the sliver in time when Jesus healed the hemorrhaging woman. In a fraction of a moment, he crossed both cultural and religious minefields with grace and tender care. He let a woman touch him—an act which in itself was scandalous—and even went so far as to associate with a woman who was permanently classified as unclean because of her infirmity. For the woman to be healed was an impressive miracle, but she also was invited to partake of the bigheartedness of God through her encounter with Jesus.

Time and time again throughout Scripture, Jesus reaches out to anyone and everyone who will listen and respond. He doesn't discriminate. His love extends to all. Sometimes I can sense him reaching out to me. You see, it's one thing to reach out to someone else, but to have a hand extended to me, well, that's somehow harder to deal with.

Such love is still intimidating to me. God's bigheartedness leaves me speechless, motionless. I can't quite explain it, but deep down inside, I feel afraid. I am scared that if I get too close to the light of God's love, it will expose all the areas in my life which are not only unlovely, but unlovable. I fear his love, but at the same time I am drawn to it. I want to know the love of the Organic God. I want to explore the boundaries and beauty of his bigheartedness. I want his love to saturate my being. My soul craves it.

Dehydrated and thirsty, I stand before the powerful waterfall of God's loving grace. I'm scared to get too close for fear of being washed away, but I desperately need the thirst-quenching water. So I take a deep breath and plunge into the floodwaters of grace — driven by an instinctive need for true love that is stronger than any fear that could hold me back. Maybe that's why the Bible says perfect love casts out fear. The closer we get to his love and experience his bigheartedness, the more the fear diminishes until we are captivated by him and no longer captive to fear.

Yet I'm amazed at how often I forget this truth and try to hide from God, rather than hungering after him and his love.

In his bigheartedness, I am finding God continually strips me of myself. He invites me to resist my own natural, knee-jerk reactions to a messed-up world and replace them with a God-designed response that transforms both me and those I come in contact with. God invites me into a never-ending relationship with him.

In the fullness of his grace, God doesn't turn us into drones or robots, but nurtures us as his children. God, above all, desires relationship with us, and in the process, we are changed to become more like him. Our own actions and reactions are softened and morphed by God's very presence. We begin to reflect the light of our heavenly Father to the world around us.

As I continue to read the words printed in red in my Bible, there's a sense that Jesus isn't providing an explanation of how to live as much as he is issuing an invitation to real life. He is welcoming us into his kingdom and under his authority, a place where the rules and guidelines of the world are turned on their head and we are invited to embark on a journey of relationship with God.

The book of Isaiah reminds me of God's bigheartedness. Tucked into the prophet's words is this fine gem:

> But now, this is what the LORD says —
> he who created you, O Jacob,
> he who formed you, O Israel:
> "Fear not, for I have redeemed you;
> I have summoned you by name; you are mine.
>
> When you pass through the waters,
> I will be with you;
> and when you pass through the rivers,
> they will not sweep over you.
>
> When you walk through the fire,
> you will not be burned;
> the flames will not set you ablaze.
>
> For I am the LORD, your God,
> the Holy One of Israel, your Savior."

Isaiah 43:1 – 3

In three verses, God manages to remind me that no matter what I have done or left undone, I am still his. He has created me and redeemed me and summons me to himself. No matter where I go, no matter what I pass through — whatever elements of this world I'm exposed to — his protection is secure. He is Lord. He is God. He is Holy. He is Savior. In my brokenness, imperfection, and sin, he whispers three holy words:

You are mine.

Somehow those words, no matter what I'm facing or going through, seem to make things better. I don't know how they do it, but somehow they bring clarity to the blurriest of situations and light to the darkest of times. Packed into those three words is redemption from the past and hope for the future. They provide purpose, identity, and most importantly, rest for my most tired innermost parts. They are luminescent — words of life from the One who gives us life.

You are mine is not a consolation prize. It's a promise.

The message is clear. God asks us to purify ourselves from the unnatural additives of the world and enter into a life-infusing relationship with him. We are urged to know ourselves, our true selves, our organic selves, in his presence; and in the process, we are changed and empowered to live the life that he has called us to.

The Organic God extends a bighearted invitation, one that

says, "I will not only go before you in this journey and make it possible—I will also go with you." Today. And every day. Something comes alive in me when I reflect on God's bigheartedness and his desire to restore relationship with us.

That alone makes me stand back in childlike awe.

The next time you find yourself asking our heavenly Father for something, don't be surprised if he answers your prayer with more than you expect. Because he may not just give you what you ask for—he'll give himself—and in the process, invite you to give of yourself to others. Like my dad, he's very bighearted that way.

.003 Breathtakingly Beautiful

My best friend in high school was Jewish. Though she was a year older than me, we were inseparable. We joined the same clubs, participated in the same activities, hung out on weekends, and shared our deepest doubts and dreams. Together we found solace from the angst of adolescence in late-night conversations over honey-laced mugs of Celestial Seasonings herbal tea.

Our heritage was one of our deepest connecting points, allowing us to share parts of ourselves that few others could ever fully understand. Take, for example, potato latkes, a staple in any good Jewish diet. To the outsider, they were mere hash browns, but to us they were a nosh of our history, an edible texture of our complex pasts. When we spoke about our lives —our quirky Jewish grandmothers, our entrepreneurial Jewish fathers, or the pressures and expectations that are inherent with being Jewish—we found comfort in knowing that we weren't alone. We promised one another that everything was going to turn out okay, that adolescence didn't last forever, and even if it did, that we still had each other.

We only had one issue that separated our hearts: Jesus. I

believed he was the Messiah; she did not. Jesus was not a dividing line initially. His name rarely came up, not because we were trying to avoid him as much as because there were so many other things to discuss. Though I didn't talk to her about God, I did talk to God about her. A lot. More than anything, I wanted my best friend to know Jesus.

One semester, she decided to start coming to our church for Sunday night youth services. I thought God was answering my prayers. We listened and learned and discussed everything, but eventually she decided that she was going to hold on to her Jewish faith. I argued that following Jesus didn't mean letting go of that faith, but rather embracing the fullness of it. She disagreed. She wanted to be a Jew, not a follower of Jesus.

A silent but powerful fissure penetrated our relationship. Though unspoken, the separation grew wider. I remember one evening she called me to talk about our different beliefs. She pointedly asked me what I believed would happen to her if she died without choosing to follow Jesus. I dodged the question, but she persisted. So I finally told her what I thought, and I can still remember the deafening silence. In that moment, she uncovered the naked truth of my heart: I was more concerned about her eternal destiny than I was about her. When she finally spoke, she asked me to stop trying to convince, convert, or coax her into believing anything different.

Our relationship lost traction. She graduated the next spring and headed to college while I finished my senior year. On the few occasions we have spent time together since then, it's not the same. Maybe it never will be. I care for her deeply and pray for her more than she will ever know, but looking back, I realize that she was right—my motives were mixed and complex. I wanted her to become a Christian more for me than for her. I wanted her to have what I had, whatever the cost. My agenda became more important than our relationship, and I became more concerned with my own righteousness than with her redemption. The salvation I was offering her was centered on myself—making her believe what I did—rather than having her believe God.

The experience still haunts me. Even today I struggle to tell people about my faith. I find myself questioning my motives, my methods, and even the message I am trying to communicate. Sure, I can write about it all day long, even speak to thousands, but when I have to talk one-on-one with someone about Jesus, my palms sweat, my voice shakes, and anything I ever knew about faith, God, or the Bible falls out of my head.

I know that God uses all kinds of wild and downright weird ways to draw people to himself, including burning bushes and bright stars in the night sky. Secretly, I'd really like him to use me.

God recently began answering this unspoken heart prayer

through a friend named Jay. We were both at an event in
Chicago with a group of leaders and pastors, and Jay began
sharing his story. After he had made a decision to follow Jesus
as a teen, his parents disowned him. Yet he felt a clear call on
his life. While praying, he felt God whisper to him that one
day he would start a church in Arvada, Colorado. At the time,
Jay had never been to Colorado, let alone started a church.

A few years later, Jay felt the same nudge again. In response,
he moved his family and a small team to Arvada to build a
community centered on what it means to follow Jesus. When
I met Jay, his church had 100 members. As I pressed Jay
for more details, he revealed something unusual: of the 100
members of his church, 75 had just committed their lives to
following Jesus. Usually when a new church launches, it has
to pull followers of Jesus from other churches just to survive
—let alone thrive. People may decide to follow Jesus as the
church grows, but they are rarely the majority of people in a
new church.

Listening to Jay's story, I reflected on my own fumbled efforts
with my best friend more than a decade earlier. I had to know
more. I pressed Jay to find out how he helped so many people
make a decision to follow Jesus. Jay said that rather than hang
out in the church, he went to where people who didn't know
Jesus spent time: the surrounding community, sports events,
bars, just about anywhere. I guess you don't have to go too

far from the front doors of a church to find people who don't know Jesus.

My interest was piqued but not satisfied. I pushed harder. What did he actually say to people when he approached them to talk about God? He said he only asks one question:

What do you love about Jesus?

His words took my breath away. I had never heard something so simple but so soul penetrating. Some say that love has no agenda, but through the experience with my best friend, I have come to believe that love is the agenda. Jay's question represented that love — not the love that seeks to be understood as much as to understand. This one question was the missing link I had been praying for when it came to sharing my faith.

As Jay spoke, my mind sifted through everything I had been learning about God. I instantly knew my answer to his question, and to this day it has not changed.

The thing that I love about Jesus is his beauty. Though the prophets tell us that there was nothing in his physical form that would attract us to him, the redemption of Christ takes my breath away. When I read through the crimson words of the Gospels, I see Jesus entering people's lives, and in only a few words or sentences, he penetrates the core of who they are, and at the same time reveals God's great love for them. The Son of God's ability to expose the brokenness of humanity and the depths of his Father's love is not just attractive but captivating.

In his interactions with people, Jesus flashed the beauty of his Father, a God who is breathtakingly beautiful. Such beauty is a reflection of his holiness, a representation of the harmony of the Trinity, and its expression is manifested throughout creation. I see this expression played out time and time again in the form of redemption. God is redeeming me—removing the stains and darkness of my own soul, and at the same time, redeeming others, revealing the beauty that is but a reflection of his own. Redemption is one of the greatest beauties we will ever encounter. For me, redemption is like a postcard from God, reminding us that he's still at work, he has not forgotten us, and he is closer than we think.

I recently encountered this redemptive beauty during a baptism I attended for a man who had no arms or legs. As his body was lowered into the water, no one mourned his physical loss—we were too busy celebrating his spiritual gain. My eyes saw a weary man wearing a stained shirt and tattered shorts, the remnants of a dismembered body, but my soul saw a vibrant portrait of God's redemption—a rich mixture of courage, hope, and strength embodied in its fullness. The beauty of that moment left tears streaming down my face. I felt that holy hush that occurs whenever heaven cracks wide open on a human life.

The more I reflect on God and who he is, the more I am mesmerized by his beauty. This beauty is more than just visual stimulation or attractiveness. While passages throughout the Bible depict God and his throne room full of textures, colors, jewels, and creatures yet unknown — those are just manifestations of a deeper truth, namely, that God himself is the source of all that is beautiful.

Our modern culture has watered down beauty to mean little more than prettiness, popularity, or likeability. We speak of the "beautiful people" as those who possess something we do not, and we cheapen beauty to a list of who's hot and who's not. Beauty is used to describe anything and everything we prefer. We're even taught to select our produce by that which looks best — namely, large and shiny — and as a result, we often pass by the organic selection. We prefer fruits and vegetables that are attractive on the outside but affected by pesticides and chemicals on the inside.

The beauty of God invites us to something different, something deeper that pushes beyond external appearance. The great theologian Augustine suggested that God alone is beautiful, good, true, and real; therefore, he is the source of all those attributes. True beauty is much more than aesthetic appeal; it's a reflection of our Creator. Yet all too often, the reflection of God's beauty becomes a distraction rather than drawing our hearts back to him.

This kind of distraction happens more often than I would like to admit, particularly whenever I'm in nature. Whether I'm walking along a beach or enjoying a rest on the soft moss in the depths of a forest, I have a tendency to be absorbed in the beauty of God's creation. My eyes dart around searching for textures, colors, contrasts. At times, I simply cannot take in the beauty fast enough. I am not just attracted to beauty, I am enamored with it. The beauty of the outdoors awakens senses inside of me I did not know I had.

This is particularly true when I encounter something new in nature. I remember as a child, my parents read of a phenomenon known as a green flash that appears at sunset. On clear evenings when the conditions are just right, the light of the sun will suddenly change color from a red or orange to green blue as it dips below the horizon. The whole event lasts only a second or two, making it difficult for the untrained eye to see the color change. As an eight-year-old, spotting the green flash was nearly impossible. But on clear nights, my father would sit out with me on the shore and loan me his binoculars so I could catch a glimpse of the mysterious light as the sun crawled into the sea.

The first few times I encountered the flash, I wasn't really sure what I saw. There was a blurred light on the horizon. Was it real or imaginary? Were my eyes playing tricks on me? Then I saw it: a sliver of green briefly pierced the horizon to display a magical light. I felt the thrill that comes with discovering a new beauty. My dad smiled with approval.

Even today when I travel, I find myself lingering for the last moments of a sunset, hoping to get just one more glimpse of the green flash. The unusual beauty is mesmerizing, and like bioluminescence, I feel the same childlike awe whenever I see it.

Such glimpses are reflections of God's beauty. Yet all too often I find myself imbibing the beauty without recognizing God. I celebrate myself for seeing the green flash, and I fail to celebrate the One who created it. I settle for the appearance of apparent beauty instead of allowing it to push my soul closer to the Creator of all true beauty. While arguably a green flash may be good and true and real and beautiful, it will never be as good and true and real and beautiful as its Creator.

In the fullness of his beauty, God invites us to change the way we look at our world. Too often I look for signs of beauty from a bottom-up perspective. I think of beauty in terms of what I prefer or what's trendy or even what feels good. The bottom-up perspective centers on me and leaves me with blurred vision unable to distinguish true beauty from merely attractive things. The Organic God invites me to take off the bottom-up lenses of this world, and asks me to embrace a top-down perspective of that which is truly beautiful. He invites me to come to him, know him, and gaze at his beauty. When I fix my eyes on him, then I can look at things in this world and better recognize which ones bear the fingerprints of the Creator. And I find myself worshiping the Maker of beauty rather than that which has merely been marked by beauty.

Maybe that's why the psalmist cries out, "One thing I ask of the LORD, this is what I seek: that I may dwell in the house of the LORD all the days of my life, to gaze upon the beauty of the LORD and to seek him in his temple."

Whatever you fix your eyes on will become your standard. As a child, my father went into the jewelry business as a side venture. I grew up sorting through bags full of various semiprecious stones, including amethysts, rubies, sapphires, and emeralds. Loose diamonds were stored individually in small white wrappers that were carefully filed and tagged according to size and quality. Occasionally, he would purchase a highly unusual piece for resale, like a hummingbird made of jewels. I loved looking at them. Sometimes I would even ask my dad to go to the bank so we could visit the safety deposit box where he stored his inventory. By the time I was in my teens, I had a pretty good eye for recognizing faux jewelry. This wasn't something I ever tried to develop or even practiced —my father just kept exposing me to the real treasures.

The beauty of God helps me see myself and others differently. I can't explain it, but when I place myself in orbit around God—where he is the very focus of my existence—I begin to recognize those things that are good and true and real and beautiful, not just to me, but to him. I begin to see people differently, recognizing the mark of their Maker, and gratitude fills my heart. I begin to see portraits of redemption all around me.

Now I don't see this all the time, or even every day, but the more time I spend with God, the more I find people that he's specifically calling me to love and serve no matter what the cost. My friend Anne is one of those people. I've known her for more than a decade, and many of those years have been marked by heartache, disappointment, and pain, as if a storm cloud follows her. I have prayed, talked, encouraged, and listened, and quite honestly, nothing has gotten any better. But when I look at her, I don't see brokenness; unexplainably, I see beauty. I see her not as she is in physical form, but as she's created to be. Instead of seeing her as a project, I see her as a projection of God's love. What I see cannot be detected by the human eye, only by eyes that have looked long and hard at God for answers. As I looked to him in prayer, I asked many questions, but he only provided one answer: *love her.* Somehow that has become enough.

I've come a long way since my fumbled relationship with my best friend in high school. I still have a long way to go, but slowly I'm discovering the transformation that takes place when we set our eyes on our breathtakingly beautiful God. He reveals what is ultimately beautiful in a way we could never imagine, and in the process we reflect a little more beauty ourselves, thus drawing others to him. We become part of the redemptive story.

I don't think it's a mistake that beauty has an unmistakable magnetic quality. Something intrinsic in humanity is drawn toward beauty. Our soul craves it. The heavens declare the glory of the Lord, and we're wired to notice such vibrant beauty.

Maybe that's why the answer to Jay's question came so quickly to me. The thing I love about Jesus is his beauty. I have always loved his beauty. I probably always will. The magnetic force of God's beauty has captivated me, and I don't want to look away.

Something changed inside my heart when it came to sharing my faith with my best friend that day. I still can't explain it, but up until my encounter with Jay, I thought sharing one's faith was a matter of coercion. Now I realize it's a matter of connection. I have something to share now that isn't about rules or religion or coaxing or convincing. I have seen something, or rather, Someone. I have caught a glimpse of the beauty of God, and I want everyone to know.

I find myself asking people everywhere I go what they love about Jesus. The answers never grow old. I have spoken to some who have been following Jesus their entire lives who deep down inside do not believe that Jesus loves them. And I have spoken with others who have not stepped inside a church in many moons, who are closer to the kingdom of God than I ever would have imagined.

The question, "What do you love about Jesus?" is so personal and percipient, that most of the time I find myself discovering new aspects of God that I had never seen or appreciated before. Each one illuminates a different facet of his beauty.

So forgive me, but I have a question that I can't not ask you,

What do you love about Jesus?

I have no agenda, except one. I promise.

.004 Amazingly Wise

On a lazy afternoon or relaxed evening, there's nothing quite like a game of Risk, Settlers of Catan, Sequence, or speed Scrabble to bond with friends and get a little rowdy. One of my all-time favorite games is Yahtzee. I love the thrill that comes with each roll of the dice. Intrigue, risk, expectation, and of course, the possibility of wildly screaming "Yahtzee!" like a semicrazed lunatic, give the game an addictive quality.

When it came to applying for college, I felt like I was rolling the dice with my applications. My Yahtzee school was Georgetown University in Washington, D.C., and if everything lined up just right, my overachieving, driven self planned on majoring in international relations and pre-law. I knew it was foolhardy to apply to only one school, so I filled out applications to three others and offered up a simple, albeit slightly dangerous prayer: *Dear God, let me know which school you want me to get into by only allowing me acceptance to one and rejection from the other three.*

Meanwhile, I did everything I could to get into Georgetown University—from asking alumni to write letters to engaging in extra-extracurricular activities to enrolling in an overpriced SAT prep course with a money-back guarantee that promised to boost your score. I can still remember the prep course teacher explaining that despite points being taken away for wrong answers on the SAT, you still have a decent chance of getting the right answer by simply responding to the questions on the test. To illustrate his point, he pulled out a deck of cards and asked us to blindly tell him whether the next card he selected would be a diamond, heart, club, or spade. He went around the room as each student selected cards — often getting 25 percent or more of the guesses correct. When it was my turn, I randomly rotated between the four options. After picking eight cards in a row incorrectly, the instructor commented that he had never seen anything like it. By the time I selected twelve cards in a row incorrectly, he said, *That's impossible.* When I reached sixteen cards in a row, he realized I was unintentionally undermining his lesson on how to take the test. He moved on to the next student.

After completing the class, I retook the SAT. My score lowered nearly two hundred points.

Neither my parents, myself, nor Georgetown were impressed. The latter issued a rejecting letter and two more schools followed suit. Only one school, Wake Forest University, offered placement on the waiting list. It wasn't the Yahtzee school I was gambling on, but within a month, an admissions counselor from the university called and offered me a spot. I gratefully accepted. God had answered my prayer, and in his wisdom, he did not give me what I wanted. He gave me what I needed.

During my time at this university, I fell in love with studying the Bible and went through that mysterious God-infused metamorphosis where my faith became my own. Could it all have happened at Georgetown? Possibly, but I would argue that it's unlikely. I think the pull of politics and the power of D.C. would have only fed the drivenness of my own soul. At Wake Forest, I was able to remove myself from the fast track and instead spend long afternoons soaking up warm sunshine listening to Dave Matthews. In four years, the biggest leadership role I accepted was cocaptain of the intramural inner tube water polo team for my sorority. We lost every game.

One can never know the great "what ifs" of life, but with such a clear answer to prayer — admittance to one school and denial to the other three — I can't help but acknowledge God's providence and wisdom that I ended up in North Carolina.

That experience makes me want to throw myself at God's feet with the humblest of all prayers, *Not my will, but yours be done.* God's wisdom, true wisdom, is essential to living the life we were designed to live. Apart from God and his wisdom, we can spend a lot of time and energy getting lost, or worse, asking for directions from people who only pretend to know the way.

While I asked for God's wisdom on which university to attend, I foolishly didn't ask for his wisdom (or anyone else's) on how to live once I arrived. I packed my first year of college with lots of As on my transcript and Bs in life, namely, beer, boys, and Ben & Jerry's. Yet God and his wisdom never left. Even in the midst of fleshly indulgences, wisdom reminded me that some lines were simply too dangerous to cross.

Following my freshman year, a youth pastor, who is still one of the best representations of Jesus I have ever encountered, encouraged me to attend a conference back home in Colorado. I sat through the sessions, listened to the speakers, and visited the booths with their colorful brochures and free candy. In between various conversations and a variety of teachings, I spent time in prayer telling God what he already knew: I needed him.

One afternoon, in the stillness of prayer, I felt a distinct but unusual thought enter my mind: *Go up to the prayer room and look underneath the tables.* The thought was so unusual that I knew I couldn't have come up with it on my own.

With only one surefire way to know if the thought came from God, I walked into the prayer room and tried to look inconspicuous as I circled around, looking under various floor-length tablecloths. I garnered a few questioning glances, but I didn't really care. I was on a mission. My quest wasn't really about what I found or didn't find. I had to know if God was real, and more importantly, if I was still his.

Under the final tablecloth, I found a Bible.

Ironically, the first thought that ran through my mind wasn't about God at all. All I could think was, *I'm not crazy!*

I breathed a sigh of relief and looked more closely at the Bible. A woman's name was inscribed on the cover, so I began asking other people if they recognized the name. When I stumbled on someone who not only knew her but had her contact information, I gave the owner a call. She had been praying that someone would find her Bible.

She lived about an hour and a half away.

As the conference came to a close, I shared the story with a few people, one of whom had been praying for a ride to a city in the direction that I was traveling to return the Bible. I didn't only find my own prayers answered, but in a very real and tangible way I became a part of answering the prayers of two others.

I still look back on that experience of finding a Bible under a table at a conference as one of the turning points in my life. Through prayer, the Organic God spoke, I responded, and I encountered the living God, a Spirit far more real than I ever expected. Through that experience, God whispered three familiar words: *You are mine.*

A spiritual hunger awoke inside of me. And during my second year of college, I began to read the Bible like never before —not just because of my hunger to know God but because of my biblical studies classes. The assignments pressed me to dig deep into not just what I knew about the Bible but what I really needed to know. By the end of my sophomore year, I was nearly halfway done with the requirements for a religion major, but I didn't mean to be so far along. I just kept signing up for classes that caught my attention, and oops!, ended up with a bachelor's in religion.

I didn't just discover new facets of God in those religion classes —I discovered them in all kinds of classes from astronomy to physics to history. One of the highlights of my time at Wake Forest University was taking a class from the famed Maya Angelou. Nearing the end of my college career, I still hadn't taken a class from the popular writer and poet laureate. On occasion I had heard her speak on campus, her deep, thunderous voice filling the auditorium and settling over the listeners like a down blanket on a cold winter's day.

Some speakers own the room; Maya Angelou owned the campus. She was never afraid to address uncomfortable topics like prejudice, discrimination, and sexuality, but she did so in a way that was both tantalizing and terrifying. While she verbally welcomed exchanges and debate, you never knew where the line was, *that* line, the one you're not supposed to cross.

Though dubbed a professor, Ms. Angelou rarely taught more than one class a semester. In the world of academia, she seemed far more like a trophy than a teacher, but no one really seemed to care. After all, she was Maya Angelou.

For that simple reason, I signed up for her class. The truth is that I didn't know a whole lot about the woman except that she was a world-famous poet and had been celebrated on Bill Clinton's inauguration day. It wasn't much, but I knew enough to know that if I didn't sign up for her class, I would regret it one day.

Now as you can imagine, rumors ran wild about signing up for a class taught by Maya Angelou. Some said it required a personal interview. Others cited an essay. Still others spun yarns of a waiting list a mile or at least several semesters long. I wasn't too surprised when the registrar's computer printed a hopeful-list notice, but I decided to join the ranks of the waiting and showed up to class on that first day.

The class was limited to thirty or so students, but less than a half dozen were on the waiting list. I was number three. Those nasty rumors about the impossibility of getting into the class had prevented many students from even trying. Ms. Angelou began the class by taking attendance. One by one she called our last names, introducing us to each other as mister or miss. To the handful of wait listers, like myself, who had showed up to class, she said that she wanted to keep the class small, but if we came back the following week, she would let us know.

I'd like to tell you that the first class I sat in on with Maya Angelou was filled with an unforgettable poetry reading and rich stories about her textured life, but for the next hour or so, we went around the room, and each student gave an introduction and clearly stated and spelled his or her name. In this class, I was no longer Margaret, I was Ms. Feinberg, and everyone else would recognize me as such.

At the end of class, Ms. Angelou explained that what we were learning was very important. In fact, it would form the basis of our first test. *Our first test?* I thought. *I should have been paying more attention.* I quickly sketched a seating map and recorded as many people's names as I could.

A week later, the poet laureate called me, Ms. Feinberg, to the front of the class. I responded with the kind of awe reserved for religious occasions. She asked me if I liked the class, to which I heartily agreed. She asked if I would attend regularly, to which I nodded my head affirmatively. Finally, she asked if I would work hard. I promised to do my best. With a priestly nod, her deep voice assured me that I was no longer on the waiting list. In fact, everyone who was on the waiting list and who showed up to class was welcomed into her classroom that day. No essay. No prolonged interview.

So much for all the rumors. I settled back into my seat, smiling.

"Now everyone, get up and change seats," Ms. Angelou directed.

My smile quickly faded; my seating map was worthless.

We spent the second class reviewing each other's names. Round and round the room we went until the class came to a close. It wasn't exactly the awe-inspiring look at African-American literature I was hoping for.

"Next week," Ms. Angelou announced, "I will set aside time for testing. You will be called on by name to identify someone else in class."

I breathed deeply to avoid a panic attack. I hated being put on the spot.

The third week of class, we endured Ms. Angelou's hour-long interactive test as we went around the room naming each other as Ms. so-and-so or Mr. so-and-so. When she called my name, I pictured the person in their original seat in class, visualized my handwritten map, and somehow said the right name. Then I breathed a huge sigh of relief and took an imaginary Valium.

At the end of the interactive test (which we all passed), she asked a simple but unforgettable question: "Why did we just spend the last three weeks getting to know each other's names?"

She pressed further: "Why did I just spend nearly 20 percent of our very valuable class time together making sure you knew each other's names?"

The room was silent in a kind of deafening, molasses-thick stillness that only someone with the presence of Maya Angelou can command.

"Because your name is a sign of your dignity," she explained. "And when you recognize someone's name, you recognize them not just as human but as a person. One of the greatest ways you bestow human dignity on someone is by calling them by name."

For the remaining weeks of class, we read a wide range of African-American literature—including works by Maya Angelou herself. We listened in reverence as she read and recited poems that shook the soul. We laughed when she shared colorful stories from her childhood, personal adventures, and experiences as an actress. We held back tears when she told of her painful past. And we all dug deep to create a final project that answered the granddaddy of all questions:

Why does the caged bird sing?

More than a decade later, the greatest lesson I learned from Maya Angelou is from those first three weeks. She did more than teach a lesson about human dignity—she allowed me to experience and partake of it firsthand. I don't remember the names of my classmates, but I still remember the sense of empowerment I felt both when I called on someone's name and when mine was called upon. After sitting in her class, I will never be able to refer to Maya Angelou as merely Maya.

This woman, whom I barely knew at the beginning of the semester but fell in love with by the end, captured my heart and imagination not because of her fame, accolades, or literary acclaim, but because she displayed such deep and rich wisdom. Maya Angelou didn't just want us to have information; she wanted us to take part in the process of transformation. She didn't just want us to know about human dignity; more than anything, she wanted us to treat other humans with dignity. In the process, she revealed the power of true wisdom.

Wisdom is more than just practical know-how. Wisdom illuminates a better way to live, and even allows us to consider the *best* possible way to live. Wisdom is so smart that it doesn't travel alone. Wisdom's companions include understanding, knowledge, counsel, discernment, discretion, justice, and equity. It's hard to find wisdom apart from its cohorts. Proverbs 2:10 declares, "For wisdom will enter your heart, and knowledge will be pleasant to your soul" and Proverbs 8:12

proclaims, "I, wisdom, dwell together with prudence; I possess knowledge and discretion."

If wisdom is the handle and fabric of an umbrella, then its companions serve as spokes, offering protection from whatever comes—rain-driven storms or the heat of the day. Like an umbrella, wisdom can also be used like a cane when the journey of life becomes steep and our steps become unsure.

I think that's one reason that when we ask the Organic God for wisdom, we get so much more. Wisdom is the gift that keeps on giving. Our amazingly wise God invites us to pray and pursue wisdom, promising that our efforts will not go unrewarded. In the process we discover that wisdom is a treasure, and we find an even greater treasure, God himself.

Scripture reveals that wisdom begins with the fear of the Lord. We are invited to obtain wisdom—a portion, any amount, no matter how small—from his storehouse. As we stare into the depths of wisdom, it enters our heart, and its presence becomes pleasant and luminous to our soul. Wisdom takes on a life of its own as it grows and comes alive within us, directing us, protecting us, and leading us into the life God intended.

God is the author of wisdom and all of its companions. The wisdom he gives has signature qualities—it's trademarked for being pure and peaceable, gentle and merciful, reasonable and unwavering to the point of producing good fruit without hypocrisy. If you follow the trail of wisdom, you can't help but find salvation, redemption, and protection along the way. The more I learn of God's wisdom, the more intrigued I become. My love and fascination of wisdom transfers itself to a natural love and fascination with God.

The wisdom of God knows no boundaries. There are no lists of taboo topics. Everything is covered — from the rich to the poor, from good to evil, and from wise to foolish. God's wisdom crawls under bushes and into caves to offer its illumination. Sometimes when faced with such light, I am the one who wants to crawl away.

I remember one particular spring semester during college when I started hanging out with a warmhearted guy. He was smart, sensitive, funny — the kind of guy you can stay up with until three in the morning talking about everything and nothing all at the same time on a grossly stained college couch that hasn't left the university in more than twenty years and decide that it's still worth staying up just a few more hours to see the sun rise even though you already have a slight headache and know the sleepless night will really hurt the next day, but you rationalize that you're in college and these are the days you'll remember, and if you can both make it to morning he will spring for the Krispy Kreme donuts.

One of those kind of guys.

Before we knew it, we were both twitterpated. We began dating, thoroughly enjoying college life together, except for one hiccup: he just wasn't that into Jesus, and he made it very clear that he wasn't going to be. We had a problem, but I was doing everything I could to minimize it. I wanted more time on the sticky college couch and another warm Krispy Kreme and at least one more late-night walk back to the dorm under star-filled nights and just a few more soft, warm kisses that made my knees buckle.

Yet deep down inside, in that place where you can't just put on a lock and throw away the key, I knew my actions were not pleasing to God. I knew I couldn't bind myself—even in a light romantic dating relationship—to someone who didn't share a passion for Jesus. My close friends knew it too. A few well-meaning ones quoted an oft-used passage about not being *unequally yoked*. I shrugged it off as oxen talk.

Soon I found myself sitting in an Old Testament class listening to a professor lecture on God's command not to marry foreign wives because of possible spiritual and moral corruption. Week after week, we kept revisiting this theme in various books of the Bible, including Nehemiah and Malachi. Meanwhile, during my personal studies, I kept stumbling on verses that echoed the same sentiments. This concept of marrying foreign wives who serve foreign gods reminded me of my own relationship with someone who didn't love the same God.

I knew I had to break it off.

But not right away. It took several weeks during which the Krispy Kremes slowly lost their flavor, the couch developed an unmistakable stinky odor, and those kisses went from soft and sweet to slightly bitter.

My heart wanted one thing, my spirit wanted another.

On an unforgettable afternoon, I took a deep, panicked breath, walked into his room, and tried to explain to him why we couldn't keep dating. I foolishly blathered about how in the Old Testament, God forbids marrying foreign wives because you will eventually begin serving their gods and how I knew he wasn't foreign and I knew he wasn't a wife, but the message still applied to me and I couldn't shake it and it was time for me to cut down on the Krispy Kremes and stop kissing him. I sounded like a deranged religious nutball, but in my heart and spirit, I was finally free.

It felt more like a wrestling match than an act of obedience, but I finally responded to God. True wisdom always begins with a deep sense that God's ways are wiser and better than our own — fear of the Lord truly is the beginning of wisdom — but that doesn't mean it's always easy. Looking back, I still don't know what I was saved from, but I know who I saved myself for, and I am grateful.

Beyond the power of God's wisdom to guide and protect us,

one of the most captivating aspects of wisdom is its simplicity. True wisdom doesn't put itself on display, like the thick volumes of rarely viewed academia that I thumbed through in college. Wisdom is not the complex reasoning of tenured professors. No, wisdom shines in quick, seemingly sudden moments of brilliance.

Consider for a moment the book of Proverbs, most written by Solomon. You would think a book on wisdom would be filled with long theoretical and esoteric arguments, but instead it's packed with quick-witted and quirky observations on life. We read about everything from health and hatred to dogs and vomit.

Here are a few of my favorites:

> *Better a meal of vegetables where there is love than a fattened calf with hatred.*
>
> Proverbs 15:17

> *Starting a quarrel is like breaching a dam; so drop the matter before a dispute breaks out.*
>
> Proverbs 17:14

> *As a dog returns to its vomit, so a fool repeats his folly.*
>
> Proverbs 26:11

> *Do not move an ancient boundary stone set up by your forefathers.*
>
> Proverbs 22:28

An honest answer is like a kiss on the lips.

> Proverbs 24:26

Like one who seizes a dog by the ears is a passer-by who
meddles in a quarrel not his own.

> Proverbs 26:17

The book of Proverbs teaches us that wisdom isn't just for the elite. Though kings and queens need wisdom, the nuggets are just as applicable to the rest of us. Proverbs is packed with wisdom that speaks directly to the newlywed couple, the chef, the real estate agent, the dentist, and even the pet owner. Whether you're looking for practical know-how on how to parent, select friends, eat properly, or deal with a loan shark, Proverbs offers practical insights and advice. Every reading of this rich book offers something new.

Recently I stumbled on this gold mine:

> Where no oxen are, the manger is clean,
>   But much revenue comes by the strength of the ox.

> Proverbs 14:4 NASB

Written in the language of a farmer, this proverb offers a powerful business lesson:

Sometimes work stinks, but keep it up because it will lead to profit.

While I love writing, I don't enjoy some aspects. I would rather go to the dentist for a root canal than develop a book proposal or align footnotes in a manuscript. This Scripture insinuates that any job worth doing has its poopy parts—whether you're a college student, a writer, a farmer, a minister, or an executive for a Fortune 500 company.

I just said "poopy." I'm officially guilty of cursing like a six-year-old.

The proverb gives listeners a choice:

No oxen = No poop = No profit   OR   Oxen + Poop = Profit

Notice that the proverb doesn't tell listeners how to live as much as it illuminates the best possible life. Like my encounter in Maya Angelou's class, wisdom doesn't impart information as much as it invites us into the process of transformation. When we embrace wisdom and its companions, we find our attitudes changed and our responses transformed.

Shoveling doesn't seem so bad after all.

Such wisdom found in the Bible has always captivated me. It has depth and texture and richness. You can read one verse a hundred times and still find something new.

I remember hearing the story of Solomon and the two disputing mothers when I was a child. Two women came to Solomon and claimed to be the mother of the same child. They told the king that they both had been living in the same house and gave birth within three days of each other. One woman's son died in the night from accidental suffocation. Now they stood in the king's quarters arguing.

Who was the real mother of the living child?

The story didn't have a clear answer. Was it mother No. 1 or mother No. 2?

Solomon asked for a sword. With the child so young, the king couldn't know which mother the child loved best, so he wanted to know which mother loved the child best. Solomon decided to divide the living child in two by giving each mother one half of the baby.

Cut a baby in half? Even as an elementary school kid, I knew this didn't sound very "Bible-like."

One of the mothers spoke up. She would rather have her child alive with a different mother than have him killed at any cost. The second mother didn't care. Solomon, in his wisdom, uncovered the untarnished truth proving the real mom. Solomon's prayer for wisdom has become my own. I don't just ask for hunger for God anymore. When I pray, I also ask God for the wisdom of Solomon. God cannot resist this simple, humble prayer. James 1:5 says, "But if any of you lacks wisdom, let him ask of God, who gives to all generously and without reproach, and it will be given to him."

So I pray, trusting and hoping that God will answer. And at moments I see him respond in full grace.

A few years ago I was speaking at a leadership conference. After I finished, a man cornered me in the hallway and asked a rather pointed question: "What gives you the right, as a woman, to get up and speak to this audience, which includes men, and talk regarding anything having to do with Scripture?"

The question took my breath away.

Before I could cognitively process the words coming out of my mouth, I answered, "Because I am his daughter."

The man looked at me, recognizing the principle that a daughter—whether on behalf of a heavenly father or a human one—has a right to speak on behalf of the family. He said, "That's a good answer."

As I look back on my simple response, I realize that it also carried a depth which was neither defensive nor offensive. I could have given many answers, both theological and theoretical, but the simplicity of wisdom rested on my lips.

God had heard my prayers.

As I look for wisdom in my daily life, I find that it often displays itself in the simplest of answers and the most concise of responses. Yet all too often, I see wisdom mistaken for clever sayings and cute quotes. These one-liners make their way into eternally forwarded emails and are even quoted on church signs and in leadership circles. You probably recognize a few of them:

- Let go and let God.
- God grades on the cross, not the curve.
- God doesn't call the qualified, he qualifies the called.

While all these contain truth, never mistake wit for wisdom. Never mistake God for an acronym (WWJD, anyone?), or worse, think that he can be summed up in one. And always beware of anything that rhymes.

Phrases like these get under my skin because even if they are fun to read, they don't require reflection. They may contain a "ha-ha" moment but no real "aha" moment. True wisdom, on the other hand, might have the ha-ha, but it always delivers the aha.

Scripture breathes wisdom like we breathe oxygen. It can't not. Through Scripture, God reveals himself. This wisdom cannot be captured, let alone contained, on a neon bumper sticker or rubber bracelet. Wisdom itself invites us to go deeper — right into a relationship with God himself.

Through wisdom, we learn to love God and love what he loves. We find rich counsel on the life we were meant for — in our families, communities, and world. We discover our personal responsibilities to others. And we unearth how to put love into action.

In an interview with Billy Graham on *20/20*, the television host asked, "If you had a homosexual child, would you love him?"

The evangelist responded without missing a beat, "I would love that one even more."

That's the kind of wisdom that quiets the critics and invites the holy hush of the Organic God.

Such a response reminds me of Jesus. As if it wasn't enough that the thirtysomething was constantly presented with the sick, mentally ill, demon possessed, poor, hungry, and spiritually lost, he was also confronted with tough theological questions from the religious leaders. Some wanted to know the truth while others wanted to trick him. Yet his responses are loaded with wisdom:

> On a question regarding tithing and taxes, *"Give to Caesar what is Caesar's and to God what is God's."*
>
> On a question of marriage and the resurrection, *"Are you not in error because you do not know the Scriptures or the power of God? When the dead rise, they will neither marry nor be given in marriage; they will be like the angels in heaven."*
>
> On his choice of dinner companions, *"It is not the healthy who need a doctor, but the sick. But go and learn what this*

means: 'I desire mercy, not sacrifice.' For I have not come to call the righteous, but sinners."

On the issue of greatness, *"I tell you the truth, unless you change and become like little children, you will never enter the kingdom of heaven. Therefore, whoever humbles himself like this child is the greatest in the kingdom of heaven."*

With the exception of answering questions about the end times, Jesus's responses are short but revealing. In just a handful of words, he exposes, enlightens, and—to borrow a line from Emeril—*Bam!* presents the truth. Most theologians would respond to such questions with volumes, but Jesus is unique in his brevity, not with a ha-ha as much as an aha.

I have the same kind of aha moment whenever I encounter God's wisdom. Whether I find it nestled in Scripture, displayed through specifically answered prayer, or demonstrated in a class taught by Maya Angelou, I can't help but stand in awe of the Organic God who is abundantly wise.

Now if only I could figure out why the caged bird sings.

.005 Surprisingly Talkative

LIKE SO MANY GRADUATES, I WAS UNSURE WHAT I WANTED to do or where I wanted to go after graduation. I thought about studying in Israel, enrolling in seminary, or digging into a program in archaeology. The possibilities of life had become like homemade pasta, and I began tossing applications in all directions to see which one stuck—praying once again that God would provide the adhesive to the place he had for me.

He did.

I was hired for a summer internship at a magazine in South Florida, where I spent several months learning some invaluable lessons, namely, that I loved writing but wasn't crazy about cubicles, commutes, or anything corporate. At the end of the summer, I still didn't know what I wanted to do with my life, but out of the blue, my parents called and invited me to go on a church partnership trip to Honduras. I wasn't too sure. Then they said the magic words: *We'll pay.*

I was in.

The weeklong trip turned into a two-month adventure, and I saved up enough money to return for an additional visit. After being robbed at knifepoint and feeling sick for weeks on end, my willingness to live overseas long-term evaporated. That's when I did what almost every graduate who doesn't know what they want to do with their life does: I moved back in with Mom and Dad.

I took a part-time job as a kids' ski instructor and began praying like crazy. *God, what do you want me to do? What are you calling me to do? What's the plan?*

I didn't hear anything. Not a peep. I was asking God one of the jumbo questions of life, and he didn't seem to have input. Though he had clearly answered prayers about getting into college and what to do immediately following graduation, he unexpectedly switched to silent mode. The God who had been surprisingly talkative was now deafeningly silent.

I continued to pray. Weeks rolled into months, and I still didn't have any idea what God wanted me to do with my life. As much as I enjoyed a spacious house and a well-stocked refrigerator, I knew I couldn't live with Mom and Dad forever. Besides, my college friends were already landing jobs at name-brand banks, prestigious law firms, and world famous hospitals.

I had to do something.

I decided to turn the question around. Instead of asking God what he wanted me to do, I began to ask myself what I wanted to do. In other words, if I could do anything with my life, what did I want to do?

I wanted to write.

The desire didn't just float into my mind like a pipe dream; it came from deep inside the core of who I was. Once I gave voice to the words *I want to write*, the desire grew even stronger. Three days, seven days, ten days passed. I couldn't shake it.

Mom and Dad graciously offered me my old bedroom for as long as I needed it. I headed to the library and began researching how to get published. The articles were depressing. They cited the percentage of wannabe writers that never get published. I shrugged off the discouragement. The internal fuel to write was greater than any fear of rejection.

I contacted a half-dozen religious magazines and asked if I, an unknown recent college graduate without a journalism degree, could write for them. All but one said yes.

Maybe God wasn't as silent as I thought.

More than a thousand online and print articles and nearly two dozen books and Bible studies later, I think God's silence was the most brilliant answer to my prayers, *God, what do you want me to do? What are you calling me to do? What's the plan?*

If God would have whispered to me that his plan for my life was writing, I would have responded out of a sense of obedience. I think that in the unique way I am wired, the sense of obligation to fulfill God's will for my life would have only taken me so far. When faced with the countless challenges and hardships that accompany professional writing, I probably would have walked away by now. In his silence, God allowed me to discover the gift that he had woven inside of me. That process has given me a deep sense of appreciation for the gift, so that I just can't walk away when things get tough. Because of God's silence, I recognize writing as one of those things I was created to do. That's why, like an artisan, I spend long hours honing my work—praying for the beauty to emerge.

But as I practice the art of listening to God, I am discovering that he is surprisingly talkative even in the silence. Prayers are not going unanswered as much as he is responding in unexpected ways. Listening to God's voice requires more than just my ears; it requires my eyes, my mind, my spirit, my entire being to recognize the God-nudges in life.

His voice is found in the wisdom of friends and spiritual leaders. He whispers through dreams and visions and abundant provision. He speaks through both conscience and conviction and an undeniable sense that some thoughts are more like God-thoughts than my own. He even speaks in the silence. In the process, I find myself both enticed and intrigued by him. I find myself hanging on every word. God's voice becomes the only voice I want to hear.

More and more that voice is becoming a lifeline, and I discovered I am not the only one who feels this way.

Most of my Bible crushes — those people whose lives I read about and want to emulate — both recognized and responded to the voice of God. From Adam and Eve in the garden to John on the island of Patmos, God revealed himself in both the subtle and the sublime. God spoke of himself, his nature, and his ways through story and song, fire and rain, donkeys and doves. He spoke through divine encounters and everyday life experiences, as well as the wise counsel of others. He illustrated his promises with rainbows and cloud-filled skies. From his first words, "Let there be light," to his closing line, "Yes, I am coming soon," God's voice sings throughout Scripture. And I want that voice making rich, textured music in my own life.

In my hunger to know God as he really is — free from the pollution of preconceived notions — I realize how much I need his voice. I need him to speak life and truth into my soul. I need him to illuminate my darkness and expose my sin. I need his words of hope and healing just as I need his words of discipline and correction. Apart from his voice, I will eventually wander my own way far from him. Apart from his voice, I will settle for lesser lovers. Apart from his voice, I cannot fall in love with him all over again.

That's why I keep coming back to the one book that continually turns up the God-volume in my life. Loud and harmonious, the Bible hums with mysterious sounds. How can ancient stories from faraway lands still speak so clearly to our modern world? The Bible is a book that's not only before, but during and after its time. The more I saturate myself in this book, the more I find that the Organic God challenges, corrects, encourages, and draws me closer to himself. All the while, I feel those mini-nudges of repentance, confirmation, and direction.

Every so often, I will find a sentence or phrase that reads as if it was written specifically for me for that day. Mark 6:31 contains one of these gems: "Come away by yourselves to a secluded place and rest a while." Within the context of this chapter, Jesus is speaking to the disciples after they learned that their friend John the Baptist had been slaughtered, but within the context of my own life, it's as if Jesus is issuing a personally engraved invitation to me.

Come. Away. A Secluded Place. Rest. A While.

Each word is loaded with personal meaning. A solicitation to leave my frantic busyness and move toward a deeper relationship with God. A challenge to slow down and take some much needed alone time. A reminder to close my eyes to the immediate demands of life in order to get a better view of the eternal. Though the invitation doesn't say how long to stay, I know from experience that resting will be well worth my while.

The Scripture comes alive. God speaks.

In my hunger to know the Organic God, the Bible is becoming more addictive. Without those pages, I cannot recognize God's voice as quickly, clearly, or with as much certainty. Within Scripture I find confirmation, direction, and balance to those faint whispers that may or may not have been from God.

Several years into my writing career, I had an opportunity to work as a freelance publicist for a large music company. I would be paid a monthly stipend that would allow me to pursue my writing career without financial concern, and I did not have to relocate, travel excessively, or work more than twenty hours a week. It was the perfect opportunity. I asked for a week to decide. They gave me less than seventy-two hours.

I began to pray—asking God for guidance, wisdom, peace, smoke signals—anything to know if I should move forward with the opportunity. The next day, as I did some much-needed vacuuming, a crystal-clear thought popped into my head. It simply asked, *Do you want bronze?*

The words felt more like a riddle than a question. *God, if that's you, what are you asking?*

I didn't understand, but I kept quietly asking the Spirit of God to reveal its meaning. Within a few hours, the message became clear in my heart, *Do you want bronze or are you willing to wait for gold?*

I knew what God was asking. The job offer was great—it looked like a golden opportunity, but it was only bronze compared to what God had planned. When the company called the next day, I turned down the job offer. At the time, it was a lot to give up, and I found myself second-guessing the decision. Had I really heard from God?

I wasn't sure, but while reading through Isaiah, I stumbled on this verse:

"Then you will know that I, the LORD, am your Savior, your Redeemer, the Mighty One of Jacob. *Instead of bronze I will bring you gold.*"

At that moment, I knew I had made the right decision. I never questioned it again. God used an unfamiliar passage to affirm my decision. I had been obedient. I'd love to tell you that a few weeks or months later an even better offer came along from another company, but it didn't. Yet in my heart, I have this sense that God was pleased with my obedience. That's something that is even better than gold.

More and more I find myself captivated not just by what God says but also by how he expresses himself. Two of my favorite moments are tucked away in familiar Bible stories. In Genesis, we read of a man directed by God to do something quite wild: build a boat among people who had never seen rain. Noah obeyed—right down to the type of lumber and building specifications of the ark. Once he, his family, and a zoo of animals were on board, something rather extraordinary happened: God closed the door of the ark behind them. That detail is easy to gloss over, but I read it like an exclamation point. Just when they were doubting or at least questioning their decision to step onto a stinky, overcrowded vessel, God tangibly reminds them that it's no mistake. God speaks.

In Exodus, we read of the mighty Passover—the evening when all the firstborn of those who do not follow God's specific instructions will die. God describes the cry during that dark night as worse than there has ever been in Egypt or ever will be again. In the middle of the story, God makes a rather odd promise: not a single dog owned by a son of Israel will bark the entire night through. Even in the silence of canines, God speaks.

If God can speak through slamming doors and silent dogs, I cannot help but wonder how many other colorful ways he chooses to express himself.

Some time ago I was listening to a preacher on the radio while driving. I have a bad habit of preferring radio preachers based on the boom in their voice rather than the bounty of their message, but this one delivered both. Using a thundering tone, he talked about idolatry, and at the end of his radio show, he challenged us to ask God to reveal the idols in our own lives.

Following the radio preacher's instructions, I prayed that God would reveal any and every idol in my life. A simple but somber thought popped into my mind:

You have more idols than you can handle right now.

I sat in sober silence and felt what I can only describe as the fear of God.

Over the next few weeks, I began thinking, praying, and asking God to put my life under his microscope. I began to see how so many things—from work and money to friendships and worry for the future—had become controlling forces in my life. I was bowing down to anything and everything but God. At the core of it all was my pride. Pride that I could handle things on my own. Pride that I didn't really need God. And worse, pride that had partnered with selfishness so that the ultimate idol I bowed to was myself. That may sound strange—bowing to self—but I started to realize that time and time again, I was quick to bend my knee to my desires rather than God's.

"Show me my idols" is a terrifying prayer, but the Organic God is faithful to answer it. Facing sin is the first step to being set free. Then God illuminates our darkness, inviting us to exchange our fallen nature for his redemptive purpose through his grace.

More recently I prayed this dangerous prayer again and found myself thinking about my friends. The thought that whispered in my heart was simply, *You're more concerned with the friendships you think you should have than with the ones I have given you.*

Ouch. When I looked at my life, I realized a hole, a sense of dissatisfaction with some of my friends. I had a wide variety of rich relationships — connections with women of different ages and stages in life, but none fit the picture of the gal I could go to lunch with to talk about relationships, life, and our favorite Food Network shows, in between fits of laughing so hard we almost pee our pants. I had always had friends like that in the past and had been praying for some time that God would send someone like that again, but no one arrived. I'll confess that I even thought of switching churches or attending a civic club in order to find one.

Yet God gently reminded me that even friends, and more importantly, the picture of what we think we need or deserve, can lead us into idolatry. They can distract us from the life God wants to give us. I'd love to tell you that once I realized my folly, I immediately found myself surrounded by girlfriends who loved hiking, lunches at a local bistro, and an occasional afternoon episode of grilling — but it just didn't happen. Instead, I found myself surrounded by women of strength, innovation, and of course, a healthy dose of humor, who helped me grow in ways that an afternoon of shopping just can't buy.

Recently I was reading the story of the burning bush in Exodus 3. Moses is pasturing a flock for his father-in-law and ends up at a mountain interestingly known as the mountain of God. An angel appears in a blazing fire in a bush. The story continues:

> So Moses thought, "I will go over and see this strange sight—why the bush does not burn up."
>
> When the LORD saw that he had gone over to look, God called to him from within the bush, "Moses! Moses!"
>
> And Moses said, "Here I am."
>
> EXODUS 3:3–4

As I read this familiar story, the phrase "I will go over and see this strange sight" caught my attention. I continued to read but kept coming back to this single line, realizing just how crucial the moment was in the life of Moses. He was about to receive a life-changing call to set God's people free. This one moment would change the life of tens of thousands of people and the history of a nation.

I couldn't help but wonder, *What would have happened if Moses kept on walking?* In other words, what if Moses saw the flames and smoke and thought to himself, "That's interesting, but what I really need to focus on right now is the flock." Would

God still have called to him? Would he still have had his moment? Would God have visited him in another way?

I do not know. I would like to think so. But I do not know.

What I do know, though, is that when we encounter something highly unusual — whether a burning bush or a repetitive dream — it's probably worth taking the moment to pursue God through prayer to find out if it's from him.

Sometimes, though, I am slow to respond. I walk right past the burning bush. On a recent early morning flight, I sat next to a man with whom I casually engaged in airplane small talk.

"So where are you going?" I asked.

"I'm going to get my daughters," he replied.

His sobriety and seriousness was striking. My interest was piqued by the sense of urgency that surrounded him. I gently asked him to explain. After his divorce, his ex-wife took custody of his girls. She had recently become unable to care for them, and the situation had become abusive. He was on a mission to save and protect his children.

I sat in silence. An uninvited thought popped into my mind: *You need to pray with him.*

The thought was fueled by a surge of energy. I knew it was a God-thought.

But I didn't respond. I saw the burning bush and kept on walking. The flight took off, flew several hundred miles, and landed safely, but somehow I couldn't get the words, "Can I pray with you?" to clear my throat. I was too afraid. When I got off the plane, I turned to the man and said, "God bless you," a lousy consolation prize for true obedience.

God spoke and I refused to respond. Later that I day, I apologized to God and spent some time praying for the man. I know God heard those prayers, but for me, it wasn't the same as if I had obeyed him in the moment.

I learned a lesson that I have never forgotten. On a more recent flight, I felt a similar nudge to ask the man I was sitting by a rather simple question: "Where do you go to church?" I took a gulp and with unmistakable awkwardness raised the question. He looked at me in awe. "Why do you ask?"

"Just curious," I smiled. That one question launched us into an hour-plus discussion about God and faith. Throughout the conversation, the man kept pausing to ask me why I raised the subject. No one had talked to him about issues of faith in years.

More and more I'm learning that recognizing God's voice is a process complete with highs and lows, successes and mistakes. Like a child learning to speak and listen, mispronounced words and misunderstandings are part of the process. That's why I like to say that God whispers. If someone is yelling, you can hear them clearly from across the room, but if the same person is whispering, you need to be near them to hear.

God whispers in order to draw us closer to him. Sometimes that means we don't always hear him clearly, but God continues to speak, inviting us into a deeper relationship with him. Knowing that God is surprisingly talkative, I live in a state of God-awareness—looking for where he may be at work, listening for how he may be communicating, and learning to obey him. Through his voice, I begin to recognize not just the handiwork of what he does, but the heartbeat of who he is.

Over the years I have purchased everything from furniture to faux art from yard sales, but I have never forgotten one item I bought many years ago: a Bible. To this day, I still can't figure out what made me buy it. Nothing was particularly special about the volume, and I didn't really need it. I just knew I wanted it. I gave the owner a single dollar and a short smile and walked away.

Later that day, I began examining my purchase. As I flipped through the thin pages, I discovered a slip of paper nestled in the book of Genesis. It simply read:

> *Mr. Ashley,*
> *I know what I'm getting into and I don't want to back out.*
> *—Tina*

Something about those words gripped my heart. Without knowing Mr. Ashley, Tina, or even the story behind her words, I was reminded of my own faith journey. In the process of following Jesus, I often don't know what I am getting into, and I am usually the first to want to back out. Tina's words challenged me. Through them, God reminded me of both the cost and commitment of following him.

As I began to reflect on this through the lens of Scripture, I began to see how God time and time again asks for all of me. The invitation to faith is to follow God into the unknown. Just ask Noah, Abraham, Sarah, Moses, and countless others. Jesus commands his followers to follow him and abide in him. He doesn't want a portion or a part — he wants the whole of our existence and being to be centered on him — even when we don't know how things will turn out. Somehow God managed to use a scrap of paper from a yard sale to speak to me and call me back to himself.

In response, I once again hand God my work, my relationships, my life. It's starting to look more and more like Tina's note:

> *Dear God,*
> *I know what I'm getting into and I don't want to back out.*
> *—Margaret*

.006 Wildly Infallible

THE TRANSITION FROM COLLEGE LIFE TO LIVING AT HOME while pursuing a writing career was fluid. I found juggling multiple part-time jobs challenging yet rewarding, and the small-town community welcoming and warm. I decided to attend an independent evangelical church not because of the music, the preaching, the lighting, or the extracurricular activities, but because it was where all my friends went.

A few years out of college, I was still attending the same church and found myself longing for something more. I had been reading the stories of Jesus healing the sick, raising the dead, and working transformational miracles in the lives of those he encountered, and a hunger welled up inside my soul. At the center of it all was a simple question:

God, are you still doing it today?

I had read about God's power, but I longed to experience it. I became so desperate, so hungry to know God, that I was willing to do anything. Three years after graduating from college and living at home, I packed up my things, moved across the country to Florida, and enrolled part-time in a Bible school.

The campus was part of a church that was experiencing a modern revival. Hundreds of thousands of people from all over the world had come to visit the nightly services. At the end of the three-hour-plus evening event which included music, personal stories, a teaching, and an invitation to know Jesus, the front of the church was filled with people literally running to turn their lives over to God.

I had never seen anything like it, and I have never seen anything like it since.

During that year at the Bible school, I witnessed story after story of God's transforming power. I met a woman who had been in a wheelchair who walked. I met a man with a deadly disease who had been healed. My neighbor was a drug lord before a radical encounter with Jesus. Now he was becoming a pastor. These stories, these experiences, breathed fresh life and hope into my weary soul.

Indeed, God is still doing these miracles today.

A part of me came to life that had been dead for a very long time. A spiritual dawn shined brightly on my soul, and I felt the wonder of God return. That faith element, the portion that says God is not just to be hoped for but believed in, came alive. I began to pray expectantly again.

At the same time I was experiencing vibrant new life, something was also dying. The Bible school had a legalistic element that was silently but powerfully taking a toll on me. From all accounts, the school began by erring on the side of freedom. A handful of students abused their privileges, and a new set of rules were created. A few more attendees abused the remaining liberties, and more rules were added. The cycle continued until rules were created for everything from clothes and hair to housing and curfew.

I struggled with a few of the more stringent guidelines but for the most part accepted them without question. I figured frumpy was a low price to pay for the ways I was growing spiritually. In addition to course requirements, the school required church attendance four nights a week, with most services running anywhere from three to five hours. During the free nights, the school hosted special services with world-renowned scholars, Bible teachers, and evangelists only a fool would want to miss. The result was that my friends and I were in church up to six or seven nights a week. I was learning. I was growing. I was also experiencing overload.

You can have too much of a good thing — even church services. By the time I realized I was burning out, I couldn't really stop because I still had to attend the four services a week. I went and spoke to a school counselor about the situation and was told that attendance was required — no exceptions.

I completed the year encouraged yet tired inside. A strange

blend of hope and exhaustion churned inside of me. My love for God had been rekindled, but at what cost?

The only way I know how to describe it is that my heart felt bruised. At least that's what it felt like once I moved away and had the opportunity to choose to go to church again. I remember walking into a service, and the moment the music began, it was as if someone pushed down on a big, deep, yellowish purple bruise on my soul. I wanted to run away. I barely lasted twenty minutes.

Outside in the parking lot, I felt the internal gravity of guilt because I didn't want to be in church. My mind told me that since I loved God I should logically want to be at one of his local meeting places, but my heart wanted to be anywhere else. Part of me couldn't be there—at least not then. I later realized that it was the same part of me that needed time to heal.

It's hard to tell people that you're not going to church. They rarely understand. You instantly get lumped into a group of people who are angry with the church, mad at God, or busy doing their own thing. I still loved God, yet whenever I got near a weekend service, all I could feel was pain.

For the next six months I kept it all to myself that I wasn't going to church. I went just enough—perhaps a quarter or half of a service—for the sake of others' faith rather than my own. I still prayed, read the Bible, and tried desperately to process all I had experienced. I took my pain to God and asked him to heal and restore my bruised heart.

Slowly he did.

Six months later I walked into a church service and took a seat at the back of the sanctuary. For some unexplainable reason, it felt good to be there. That's when I knew my bruise was finally healing.

I still can't put into words how God healed me, but during those months when I was not in church, I wrestled with him in thought, prayer, and study. I knew in my mind that church was more than a denomination, a building, or a program, but God was awakening in my heart the reality that the church is the gathering of followers of Jesus. To fall in love with church meant falling in love with God's people. And falling in love with people meant putting my own preferences aside when it came to details like the style of music, the length of the service, or even the takeaway value of the sermon. During those six months, in my humility, sin, and pain, I realized that I was part of a greater story, part of God's story, his plan for redemption which was being worked through saints around the world. God the Healer was doing his work in me. When I could walk into a church without feeling any traces of the pain, I knew that God, in the fullness of his grace and restoration, had healed an area inside me I could only identify by an internal sense of discomfort.

I believe that most people will experience a bruised heart at some point in life. Some bruises are caused by circumstance. Some by poor choices. Some by sin—our own or someone else's. And some bruises are the result of living in a fallen world.

Regardless of the cause, those bruises—whether from childhood or adulthood—can remain hidden until the right set of circumstances, the appropriate amount of pressure, or the perfect personality come along, and we feel the sharp pain we had been trying to ignore.

God will often use the church to expose that pain behind our bruises. For some, the pain may actually surface during a church service. A song lyric, a story, a Scripture verse, a phrase from the sermon, or the actual service itself reminds us of our woundedness. For others, it may be an interaction with someone else within the church. We find ourselves biting our lip to the pain of the past and of sins long hidden away.

No matter what causes the pain to surface, I believe its presence is actually a gift from the God who redeems. The pain acts as a wake-up call that it is time to begin the process of healing, repentance, and forgiveness. The pain asks us to make a leap of faith—that no matter what has happened, nothing is beyond God's redeeming power. He can heal the deepest wounds. He can restore the most messed-up lives. He can reach into the darkest corners of our past and shine his redeeming light.

We are invited to believe in a wildly infallible God.

I love that word *infallible*, because it describes someone who is incapable of erring and incapable of failing. Within that frame, only One fulfills both requirements.

He makes no mistakes. He will never fail.

Our God is wildly infallible.

Nothing is beyond his redemption. Nothing is beyond his restoration. Nothing is beyond his healing power. Not the bruises. Not the scars. Not the pain.

And that really is wild! If God were wrong even some of the time, I wouldn't trust him enough to obey him. I might ask his opinion on a matter from time to time, but follow his edicts or respond to his whispers? I don't think so. But God is wildly infallible—in every way—and because of his infallibility, I can walk by faith into a land that contains the substance of things hoped for and the evidence of things not yet seen.

Now just because God does not make mistakes does not mean that we don't live in a fallen, mistake-filled world. We live in the wake of sinful actions and their consequences. We live with a sinful nature that must be wrestled to the ground every day.

And we live with the unspeakable ache that there is another place, a bruise-free zone we are waiting to call home.

Yet even in the midst of so much imperfection, our God remains perfect. His wildly infallible nature becomes something we cling to and encourage others to grab on to when the storms of life leave us beaten and stranded onshore.

I recently met an elderly woman who had obviously weathered some storms. She had just finished serving as a missionary in China and shared with me the hope and expectation of all that God was doing in the church overseas. She spoke of their fervent prayers and their faith under persecution. But when she spoke of the church in our country, her face fell. She commented on our materialism and concern for self-preservation. She noted our lack of spiritual discipline and complacency. She pointed to our lack of faith and preoccupation with worldly goods. I listened patiently, and on some level, I agreed with her observations. More than two hours later, she was still going strong, and I had heard enough.

Now I'm not naïve. I realize the church in America is far from perfect and in many ways has gone astray, but the church is still the bride of Christ. She may have holes in her dress, stains on her shoes, and smeared makeup on her face, but at the end of the day, she is still the bride. When we recognize that God's perspective of the church is not necessarily our own, then we will begin treating her with the respect and care she deserves.

We will begin building her up to what she is meant to be instead of tearing her down.

I gently reminded the woman of our wildly infallible God. Not only is he constructing a mysterious, invisible spiritual temple which he is assembling in our midst, but his handiwork is also seen in the physical church, the assemblies of followers of Jesus coming together on a regular basis to be a tangible expression of God-life to the world. Anyone with a pulse can point out the ragamuffin qualities of a local assembly, but if you spend too much time focused on the stains, then you'll soon lose focus on our wildly infallible God. He is far more concerned with his church than you or I or a hundred pastors put together will ever be. He has a plan. He makes no mistakes. He will not fail.

The more I read the Bible, the more I am convinced of God's infallibility. From a human perspective, the cross looked like the ultimate attempt to thwart his plans, and yet it failed miserably. Through Jesus's death we have redemption.

Yet despite God's wildly infallible nature, I don't always choose to listen or obey him. The book of Matthew tells of a rich young tycoon who approaches Jesus for his perspective. He asks Jesus a simple but penetrating question, "Teacher, what good thing must I do to get eternal life?"

Jesus instructs him to obey the commandments. The tycoon presses further. Jesus provides an abbreviated list: do not murder, do not commit adultery, do not steal, do not give false testimony, honor your father and mother, and love your neighbor as yourself.

The young man had kept them all, but still something pulls at him. He can't let go. He asks, "What do I still lack?"

Jesus replies, " 'If you want to be perfect, go, sell your possessions and give to the poor, and you will have treasure in heaven. Then come, follow me.' When the young man heard this, he went away sad, because he had great wealth."

I think it's fascinating that when asked which commandments the young man needed to obey, Jesus refers to the bottom six of the Ten Commandments listed in Exodus 20. He skips past the first four — all of which deal with centering your life around God — and focuses on the commandments that deal with our relationships with each other.

Only when the tycoon presses Jesus with deeper questions does he uncover his own heart issue. He loves the goods — his material possessions — more than God.

The tycoon really wanted to know what Jesus thought. He wanted instruction from the rabbi. He wanted his perspective, but he didn't want it bad enough to actually do something with it once he got it.

The Scripture abounds with God's wildly infallible wisdom

and insights, and like the tycoon, God wants to answer our questions as we pursue him through study and prayer. Yet it's possible to ask God about an issue that could change us forever, and after receiving the answer, still walk away from the transformational process. That's why Romans 12:2 reminds us to not be conformed to this world but rather transformed by the renewing of our minds. You can know God's perspective and still not do anything with it. This kind of thinking leads to the worst possible religious life — one that welcomes hypocrisy and self-righteousness.

I wonder how often I am like the tycoon. I pursue God through prayer, asking what's really going on in a situation, but once I uncover the core issue, I move on in a been-there, done-that, nontransformational kind of way. Or worse, I wonder how often I'm like all those who followed Jesus from a distance and never bothered to ask for his perspective at all.

As I reflect on what the Scripture reveals about God, I find myself needing him all the more. I cannot transform myself. As I move closer to his Word, I am faced with prejudices, biases, and opinions that are anything but God-infused. Many of them are based on my own experiences, encounters, and even wounds. In fact, when I take a deeper look at the darker parts of my soul, I find that a surprising number of my opinions and attitudes are shaded by sin and the pain of a bruised heart.

Take, for instance, the issue of giving and the church. I believe in financially supporting a local congregation, and I'm convinced that ten percent is a good starting point. A list of Scriptures would back up those beliefs. Yet when a leader gets up in front of a congregation and makes a long-winded plea for money, I begin to shrink back. I want to give. I do give. But please, don't press the issue too far, because my heart has been bruised.

While living at home with my parents, I managed to save up some money for a team of people who needed funds to drill water wells and meet the needs of the poor in a Third World country. Within twelve months, I discovered the money never went where it was intended. The funds were just gone. Gone where? I still do not know. All I know is that the gift never reached those it was meant to serve.

I might have healed more quickly from this experience if it hadn't repeated itself. Not too much later, I wrote checks to people planning to go overseas who never went on their trips, and I gave money to nonprofits who did not spend it as promised. The result was a growing woundedness and hardness in my heart. In order to protect myself, I made a quiet decision not to give to those who asked. That way, if they didn't spend the money as designated, I couldn't be hurt again.

I know I am not the only one who has been hurt in this area. I have seen people get up and walk out of churches never to return if a pastor preaches on giving or tithing—let alone plans a series of sermons on the topic. I don't think the majority of these people leave because they're stingy as much as because their heart has been bruised. Any rational person knows that in a sizable church, everything from salaries to electric bills must be paid. Yet some still walk out.

I would like to think I'm different, but I'm not. I may not leave the building. I tithe. But internally I shut down. I shrink back. If I get really honest with myself and my checkbook, I am far more likely to give to those who are in need but don't ask for money than to those who do. The pain of my wounds takes precedence over potential obedience.

The Organic God calls me away from such self-protective behavior. He exposes my bruised heart so that he can heal it. He uncovers the sinful, willful, and disobedient nature which I constantly have to battle. He shows that when I am unwilling to forgive, let go, or move on, my perspective is naturally affected, tainted, and skewed by sin. When my heart has been bruised, I'm more likely to develop a belief without consulting him, and I miss out on a deeper, fuller revelation of the truth in the situation. More importantly, I miss out on embracing the truth that in everything, he is wildly infallible.

Without his healing and forgiveness, my opinions become reactions, and in the process my spiritual life becomes more like a pendulum swing than a faith journey. The Organic God invites me to step off the pendulum and into a deeper, more balanced relationship with him—where the way I live and respond is based on his guidance, his leading, and his wisdom rather than my own. He asks me to let go of the sin and live in response rather than reaction. This can only happen when I uncover my bruises, repent of my fallenness, and allow God to heal and restore.

Within a year of pursuing a career in writing, I felt a bruise that had surfaced deep within my soul. It manifested itself in the form of self-doubt, the idea that I could never become a professional writer. I immediately knew where it came from: a high school English teacher.

During my senior year, I had a teacher who was harsh and critical of anything I committed to paper. She had a reputation for such behavior. Maybe it was a feeble attempt at negative motivation, but regardless, her words bruised my sensitive soul. Nothing that I wrote was good enough. The teacher went as far as discouraging me from entering essay contests because there was no way I could ever win. When it came to the Advanced Placement (AP) tests, she actually advised me not to waste my parents' money, I didn't have a chance. I consistently earned low marks in her class.

For whatever reason, I refused to listen. The feisty Margaret emerged when it came to writing, and I wasn't going to take her word on the matter. I entered those essay contests anyway, and through the patient proofreading of a kinder, younger teacher, won multiple contests, several thousand dollars, and a trip to the nation's capital. I took the AP and earned the highest possible score. And I found the one loophole in her grading system: any student who won the annual local magazine writing contest would be guaranteed an *A* in her class. I slyly asked if she was on the judging panel, and when she said it was completely objective, I knew I had a chance. I took it.

She was forced to give me that *A*. I smiled at the accomplishment but also felt the swelling of pain inside. Why was she so discouraging? Why was she so mean? The bruise took its toll and, unrepentant, I chose to talk about her meanly, vindictively, and unkindly out of the hardness of my heart. The Bible has a word for that kind of behavior; it's called *slander*.

A year into my writing career, my unresolved anger surfaced in the form of self-doubt and fear of failure. I noticed the thoughts, the doubts, and the fears staining my writing. I began to pray. I felt what I can only describe as the grossest response from God—he wanted me to ask forgiveness from her.

After all that she had done, I was the one who needed to

repent. I put it off for several weeks, but eventually I caved into the conviction and knocked on her door. She was surprised to see me. After a few minutes of small talk, I apologized for all the unkind things I had said about her. She graciously forgave me but was unmistakably puzzled by the experience. I don't think anyone had ever offered such a humble or poorly worded request. She asked me to forgive her for anything that may have caused me to say such things. I did and then I moved on, way on, further on than I had ever been.

I could sense that God was pleased with this act of obedience, and I noticed that the area in my soul that had been tender to criticism about my writing was now healed. I could take whatever an editor had to say and actually learn from it.

I'm slowly discovering that God's wild infallibility is actually an invitation to obedience; in fact, his infallibility makes me want to obey him all the more. His perfection exposes my own imperfection, his wisdom uncovers my own foolishness, and his infallibility reminds me of just how fallible I am.

He alone can be trusted. It's the entryway into the best possible and most costly life — the one he designed from the beginning of time. Most people spout off an opinion and that's the end of the matter. When God reveals his panoramic perspective, it's only the beginning. He sees in and through all things. His perspective is truth. Like the tycoon, we are given insight into what God thinks so that we will think like him. He invites us to action. God's truth, if taken seriously, will not just transform our minds and hearts but also our behavior. It will become action points for obedience.

Now obedience is not easy. The word itself has challenged most people since they were children. At times, the concept of obedience can still make me wince. Yet obedience in relation to God makes all the difference. Those who obey God walk in wisdom. Those who disobey play the fool. Those who obey build their house on the rock. Those who don't build on sand. That's why knowing God's truth is not enough. We must respond. And that's why I have not given up on seeking the healing I need in my own life. It's also why I haven't given up on the church. That's why I still attend, get involved, and am committed to making a difference. It would be easy to walk away, but I just don't think that's God's wildly infallible perspective on the matter.

Heart bruising will undoubtedly take place.

But I strongly believe the human heart can be restored. I believe in a God who bandages and heals. I believe in a God who uses the broken and weak to do great things. I have strong opinions about these things. Maybe you do too.

God isn't a fan of shortcuts when it comes to spiritual growth. God places us in positions that are sometimes tougher than we would naturally choose, but they're designed to make us stronger and healthier than we would otherwise be. I may not always like it, but more and more, I'm reminded that it's not so much about what I think as it is about what he thinks. He is the infallible one. And I, sadly, am not.

In the end, the panoramic perspective of our wildly infallible God is the only one that matters.

.007 Outrageously Generous

I HAVE MORE THAN A FEW GIRLFRIENDS WHO CAN DESCRIBE the details of their dream wedding right down to the lace fringe on their wedding dresses. They not only know the person they want to officiate the wedding, they can name the location, time of day, season of year, and corresponding colors —all without a prospective groom.

I was never one of those women.

Not just because I'm not a froufrou gal, but because marriage was one of those things I held in quiet contempt. I had heard too many friends bemoan the aches and pains of adjusting to married life. A handful had already called it quits, and others spoke of their spouses with a sense of lifelessness that chilled my soul. Who would want to sign up for that?

Though my parents had modeled a solid marriage for more than three decades, I saw them as the exception rather than the rule. Until my late twenties, I rarely went to bed with wedding bells dancing in my head. Then, sometime around my twenty-seventh birthday, I woke up with a desire to be married. I'm still not sure what caused it—whether spring was in the air

and everything was in bloom except me or the realization
that the big 3-0 was just around the corner — but I suddenly
wanted to travel and write and live with someone whom I
could share the memories with for a lifetime. I began to pray.

Within a few months, my aunt called from Sitka, Alaska.
My uncle had died unexpectedly while scuba diving and she
needed someone to help caretake their bed and breakfast for a
few weeks. I jumped at the opportunity. We had an amazing
time together — baking scones with freshly picked berries,
brewing large pots of Raven's Brew coffee, and exploring the
natural wonders of Alaska. She asked if I would return the next
summer.

During my second summer in Alaska, as I was signing copies
of *God Whispers* at a church café, a 6'8" guy named Leif
(pronounced Lay-ph) came in and bought two copies. Using
my gift of being strikingly unobservant, I didn't notice him.
Leif, however, noticed me, and we began hanging out in a
group together. I was clueless of any hues of romance until
my aunt pulled me aside and said, "This guy really likes you."
Oh. We eventually began hanging out more, and at the end of
the summer, he asked me to move to Alaska with the intent of
pursuing a relationship to become his wife.

I said no.

I didn't want to live in southeastern Alaska. Ew. The land

where it rains three hundred days a year. The land where it's dark up to eighteen hours a day. The land where the only Target is at the rifle range.

A month or so later, my mom met Leif at a wedding. Much like her daughter, she is not a woman to mince words. She told me I was dumb not to give the relationship a chance. I packed my belongings and made the trek from Colorado to Alaska. We were married less than a year later.

Looking back, all I can think is, *why didn't I do this sooner?* Somehow I missed the memo that marriage is better than Godiva. When I finally said "I do," I was actually bracing for a crash landing — helmet in hand — but ill-prepared for the incredible heights that accompany the holy metamorphosis of two becoming one. A good marriage is one of the great *wahoooos* of life. Now that doesn't mean there won't be turbulence or a few days when you won't feel tempted to reach for the nearest portable flotation device, but as an adventure seeker at heart, I can't deny that marriage is one of the best possible expeditions.

You never know what's around the next corner.

Take, for instance, Valentine's Day this year. The night before the heart-shaped holiday, I was lying in bed with my husband, and he asked me what I wanted as my gift. Without hesitating, I replied, "a homemade card." After all, it was part of my childhood—it was how I was brought up. Besides, a card was quick, easy, and inexpensive. It was the thoughtful gift to request.

Then, with a gulp, I realized I had to return the favor. "What do you want for Valentine's Day?" I asked. I knew it was going to be a busy day for me. We were both leaving on simultaneous business trips the day after Valentine's, and our schedules were loaded with errands to run and work to be done. I guess I was hoping that he would take the hint and we would exchange homemade cards. Or maybe he would opt for a bouquet of balloons. Or maybe something as simple as a big, wet kiss that would melt him at the knees.

"I'd like a red velvet cake," he replied.

Double gulp. "Delivered to work?" I volunteered.

"That would be great."

My mind began racing. *How am I going to pack, finish up all my projects, run errands, and still find time to bake and deliver a cake?* I had no idea how I was going to pull it off, but I knew I couldn't let him down. This was Valentine's Day, after all.

The next morning I woke up early and went online to research recipes for red velvet cake. Ingredient list in hand, I headed for the grocery store and found the place filled with people buying last-minute gifts. I muscled my way over to the cake aisle and found the ingredients. Thankfully, they'd dedicated a quick checkout line to the Valentine's Day shopper, and I quickly lined up behind four people with bouquets. Shopping done, I threw my packages in the car and raced home to begin baking. By 9:00 a.m., I had a cake in the oven. Everything was on track for a noon delivery.

At 9:45 a.m. the timer rang, and I peered into the oven. Unfortunately, my two nine-inch round cakes had kept rising until they looked like rolling hills. Still feeling confident that I could salvage the cake with the double-size tub of icing I had purchased, I used a butter knife to carefully apply the sugary substance, but with every brush I found myself tearing the cake apart. I was quickly forming a red and white glob, I was out of icing, and the cake was only half covered. Worse, I had less than half an hour before I had to deliver my Valentine's gift.

Grabbing the cake and a butter knife, I headed back to the grocery store, where I found even more people like myself (okay, not quite like myself) running around buying last-minute Valentine's gifts. I bought another double-container of icing and opted for a red helium balloon and a card just in case the whole cake thing didn't work out.

On my way to Leif's office, the helium balloon bumped up against my head. Evidently it liked what it found, because it started to nuzzle me—rubbing up and down on the side of my head, creating static, and lifting the hair on the right side of my temple. As many times as I tried to push the balloon away, it returned, and for the safety of all the other people on the road, I finally just gave in to its unwanted advances.

By the time I arrived at Leif's workplace, I was frazzled and my hair was a mess. With no time to lose, I began icing the cake in the trunk of the car, hastily filled out the card with an endearing message using an old pen from underneath the car seat, and patted down my ridiculous-looking hair. I took a deep breath, tried to relax, plastered a smile over my slightly stressed demeanor, and walked into his office with gifts in hand.

Only he wasn't there.

Yeah. Happy stinkin' Valentine's Day. He was tied up in a meeting and I had to run to another appointment, and all I could think was, *Is he going to notice just how much icing is on this cake?*

As the afternoon wore on, I began to second-guess whether or not my husband would feel loved through my feeble attempt at baking a cake. Partially driven by guilt and partially motivated by fear that he wouldn't feel loved, I decided to print out some expressions of love on the computer. I cut them out into heart shapes and placed several of them on every stair between the entryway and our second floor so he would see them when he came home.

Leif had to work late. By the time he got home, a power outage had taken out all the electricity in the surrounding area. Walking up the stairs, he couldn't see a single note. I felt like I was caught in a bad episode of *Seinfeld*.

We sat on the couch in the dark on Valentine's Day and found out something new about each other: neither of us really cared a whole lot about the holiday. He had bought flowers, made a handmade card, as well as purchased store-bought cards so I would feel loved, and I became a renegade baker with frizzy hair to express my love, even though both of us already felt thoroughly and sufficiently loved because of the way we treat each other and live life together the other 364 days of the year.

The one day of the year when our expression of love—the act of giving—was forced or at least given a retail-driven purpose, we both felt a sense of guilt and fear: what would the other person think?

When I step back and honestly reflect on my relationship with God in regard to giving, I find that many of my gifts —including tithes and offerings—have become a lot like Valentine's Day gifts: at times, much of my giving feels forced. Sometimes it's even motivated by guilt or fear rather than gratitude.

When I look really deep down, there's a more penetrating question that I wonder about:

When is it enough?

In other words, how much does God want me to give? To put it in Valentine's terms, does he want balloons, flowers, and a cake, or would he be satisfied with a card? And what if my gifts look more like doily-covered construction paper and globs of icing than a store-bought card and bakery-designed cake? Will God be satisfied? Will he be pleased?

As I reflect on such questions, I recognize how ridiculous they must seem — not just theologically but practically. The all-powerful, all-knowing God of the universe has it all covered. He owns it all. He is fully satisfied and fully pleased. (Though I have a hunch that he loves handmade cards.) Still my guilt and fear remain, and I find myself living the Valentine's Day scenario through my words and actions — cutting up hearts to leave on the stairs — just in case what I've done is not enough. It's only a short jump from wondering if I have *given* enough to wondering if I *am* enough.

Such thinking has only one thing in mind really: me. The journey to know the Organic God calls me out of such a self-absorbed and self-reliant view of reality. God invites me into something more.

He invites me into his love. Not just his big, thick, strong-armed love, the kind that redeems the world, but into all of what God loves. Scripturally, some of those things are fairly obvious. Peace is good. Strife is bad. Purity is good. Adultery is bad. Truth is good. Liars, well, let's just say they're real bad. Yet when it came to things that God loves, the list shrinks tremendously. A passing reference that God loves the *sanctuary* is found in Malachi 2:11, and of course he loves people. But in the entire New Testament, only one verse clearly and succinctly reveals what God really loves.

Second Corinthians 9:7 says, "God loves a cheerful giver."

That tiny verse says a whole lot, because God isn't as concerned with the type of gift as much as he is with the attitude behind the gift. That means that it doesn't matter whether the gift comes from Wal-Mart or Williams-Sonoma. It doesn't even matter how it's wrapped (which is a good thing for those of us who stick to the ever-ready, ever-safe gift bag). God looks at the heart, and he searches for a happy one—a person who gives out of joy rather than out of guilt or fear or even mere obligation—even when it takes a little nudging and maturation.

Why is God more concerned with the heart behind what we give rather than the actual gift? Because when we give joyfully, we reflect him. We engage in a part of who he is, what he does, and what he's all about. Since the beginning, God has been giving, and he has been doing it with a cheerful heart. It is a joy for him, and he wants to share that joy with us.

Indeed, God is outrageously generous.

Consider creation for a moment. God could have been stingy in his design. We could be living in a flat, two-dimensional, sterile world with only two colors, black and white. We could be living in a world without wonders like comets, sunrises, mountain peaks, and snuggling puppies, but instead, God designed the world in technicolor. He painted the skies with unimaginable colors and hues that constantly change. He filled the seas with life indescribable, some of which scientists are still trying to discover and understand today. He packed the planet with furry, spiky, and scaly animals of all sizes and demeanors. His creativity even leaked into the very particles that are being explored today through giant microscopes. Anyone who has watched the *Discovery Channel* for very long knows that God is wild in his design. Through the stars that fill the sky and the ocean that lines the horizon, he generously shares creation with us. Whenever we enjoy nature, we are enjoying one of the great gifts of the Organic God.

I think giving is a lot like prayer. It doesn't change God. It changes us.

When was the last time you gave a gift that made a difference in the life of someone else? Odds are that you walked away with a sense of satisfaction that money can't buy. When we give generously and cheerfully, we experience an innate sense that what we have done is good. I think that feeling was placed there by God to encourage us to engage in the act of giving even more. Think about it for a second. Giving, the cheerful kind, could take place without any internal reaction or response, but every person I've talked with who has given to someone else describes a similar sense of glee—a satisfaction. God didn't just give to us, but he also hardwired us to give.

In the process of giving—whether it's time, money, or service—our gifts can become prayers and acts of worship as we give up to God in physical form what we have already given him in spiritual form: our hearts.

The invitation to give extends beyond name-brand purchases and well-wrapped gifts from Overstock.com or eBay. We are invited to be generous in our relationships. We are invited to partake in the fellowship of love, and give of ourselves through our time, gifts, and talents. Ephesians 5:1–2 goes as far as to say, "Be imitators of God, therefore, as dearly loved children and live a life of love, just as Christ loved us and gave himself up for us as a fragrant offering and sacrifice to God."

The invitation is imitation.

God demonstrated how he wants us to live through Jesus, not as people living merely for ourselves, but as those living for something greater. We are generous in our relationships when we choose inclusion over exclusion, forgiveness over a grudge, and righteousness over merely being right. In our relationships, we get down and dirty in the practice of giving. In our relationships, we are given another opportunity to reflect and further resemble God.

Despite such high props for generosity, giving is still slow to catch on as a way of life. In the gospel of Mark, we find Jesus and a crowd of five thousand in a desolate area. The Bible says Jesus felt compassion, and he generously spent his time and energy teaching the people. As the day grew long, the disciples encouraged Jesus to send the people away so they could buy food for themselves. Jesus offered up a simple challenge: "You give them something to eat." The disciples responded by asking a question that we all ask from time to time, "How much is this going to cost us?"

In response, Jesus asked them to consider what they had, not what they didn't. He asked them to take inventory, and with the five loaves and two fish donated by a child, everyone was fed. The generosity of God is demonstrated once again. God provides.

Yet in spite of the evidence of God's provision, we still ask,

How much is this going to cost us? Such thinking reveals that we have forgotten a very simple but powerful principle: everything comes from God, including the ability to produce wealth. There's a tendency to chalk up financial success to hard work, creativity, ingenuity, and timing—and while all are essential ingredients, the real source is God. But when we think about *our* wealth, success, or stuff apart from God, then the question naturally arises, *How much is this going to cost us?* This *me* focus instantly transforms giving from opportunity to obligation.

While I agree it's true that God should get our best and not our leftovers, giving that is forced or always counts the cost quickly loses its joy. When you focus more on what is being taken from you than what has already been given, you'll quickly lose the wonder that comes with giving.

So how does joy become a natural extension of our giving? It isn't just by believing that everything is God's. That's true. Cheerful giving goes one step further by recognizing God as provider not just in belief but in action. It moves us from merely acknowledging the words, "The earth is the LORD's, and everything in it, the world, and all who live in it" to actually living with this mind-set.

We are reminded that the things we see and touch really are only temporary. Something strange happened back in the desert with the Israelites that I can't quite get away from. The

Israelites were instructed to gather as much manna as they needed to eat. Exodus 16:17 tells us that some gathered much and some gathered little. In modern-day terms, some could be classified as overachievers and others as slackers, but that didn't really matter in God's eyes. He was abundantly generous to all. The passage reveals that when they measured the manna, "He who gathered much did not have too much, and he who gathered little did not have too little. Each one gathered as much as he needed." Everyone was provided for by God.

God's abundant generosity = Our perfect provision

Some of the Israelites didn't really trust God's provision, and they decided to store up the manna for the next morning, despite the promise of God's faithfulness. When they awoke, they found the day-old manna rotten and full of worms.

I used to think that was just the kind of story found only in the Old Testament, but a few years ago, I went through a period where I felt God nudging me to do and give, but I wasn't willing to share, compromise, or take a risk. I had a sweater that I loved, and I loaned it to a friend on a cold day. At the end of the visit, I felt this gentle nudge inside that said, *Give it to her.* I took a second look at the beautiful sweater and thought to myself, *That couldn't be God.* The next day, I was with a different friend who complimented me on my new pair of gloves. Again, I recognized a nudge from God, *Offer them to her.* I refused. A few days later, I was with some friends and enjoying a box of gourmet baked goods. I remember feeling that same nudge, *Give them away.* I looked at the remaining treats and thought how awkward it seemed to offer the few pieces that were left to take home.

My selfishness didn't become readily apparent until a week or so later, when within a twenty-four-hour period, I managed to ruin the sweater with a permanent stain, lose one of the gloves, and open the box of gourmet treats only to discover they were all moldy. When I looked at the brown-turned-green delights, I realized my selfishness and stinginess. God had been asking me to take a risk and trust his provision in my life, and I had refused. The realization was so clear that I promptly spent some time in prayer, admitted my selfishness, and asked to be changed. I wanted a new heart. I wanted more than a heart that gave, I wanted one that could give joyfully.

God has slowly been answering that prayer. At times I foolishly hold back that which should be freely given, or I am tempted to give for the wrong reasons, but slowly I'm finding more joy in generosity. I am discovering that the Organic God doesn't just want me to give until it hurts, but rather to give until it feels good. If I wait until I am in the mood to give, it might be awhile. If I go ahead and give out of obedience or in response to a need, joy usually follows.

I am also realizing that my attitude and actions reveal a lot about what I really think about God. Do I see God as a giver or a taker? If I view God as a giver, then I can't help but become more generous, but if I quietly see God as a taker or begrudging in any way, then I will hold on to my possessions with a firmer grasp. My giving exposes what I really believe is the true source of all the things I possess—everything from time and money to clothes and cars. If I think everything comes from my own labors and work, then I will be slower to give than if I recognize that all good things—including material things—come from God.

In my search to understand the Organic God, I am discovering that he doesn't invite us into his generosity to take something away from us as much as he wants to give us something that we can't get any other way. When we give freely, we become more free ourselves. We become less attached to the things of this world and more attached to the world to come. We make the transition from having an inward focus to having an outward one, and in the process we reflect the radiance of our Creator.

Reflecting on all the gifts that God has given me, Leif remains one of my most precious treasures. The thing I love about marriage is that you don't get the fullness of the gift in a single moment. Rather, marriage is like an enormous gift box with countless layers. Just when you unwrap one layer of the gift, there's still another and another and another and, well, I'm not convinced the box really has a bottom. I've talked to women who have been married for decades and they still mention little things about their husbands they just learned that week—a like or dislike, a hidden allergy or health condition, or even a story from their life that remained untold.

One of the other things I love about our marriage is how different we are from each other. We have nicknames for each other: anchor and orbit. While Leif enjoys staying home on a Saturday afternoon reading books, playing *Call of Duty* on the PlayStation, or napping on the couch, I would rather explore uncharted mountain trails, pick wild raspberries, or kayak to the glacier. Paired together, he takes a lot more hikes (on well-charted trails), and I take a lot more naps. Together, we balance each other, and our lives are enriched.

As much as I recognize the beauty in the mystery of marriage, I am fully aware that at times, Leif and I must look like an odd couple from the outside. The fourteen-inch height difference doesn't help. Recently, in a self-conscious weak moment, I asked God, *Why can't we just look like every other normal couple?*

And I felt God respond, *Who are you to critique my portrait?*

For a brief moment, I had become an ingrate. I forgot that in the holy metamorphosis of marriage, God generously takes two lives and creates a single portrait meant to reflect his beauty, his wisdom, his glory—and of course, his generosity.

So I continue to unpack the gift box, and along the way, I still humbly ask God about some of the different layers. *God, how does this one fit? Where did this one come from? Why did you put this in the box?* And I hear the gentle whispers, *You'll see. It's part of my purpose. You'll need that later on.*

.008 Unbelievably Stubborn

One of the reasons Leif says he originally fell in love with me is because of my spunk. That's the non-Jewish term for chutzpah. I never thought of chutzpah as a love magnet. I always considered it a repellent. It's something all of my Jewish family members were born with and could never get rid of—no matter how hard they tried. Chutzpah means you think for yourself, you're willing to disagree, and you're brave enough to give voice to what you believe. Chutzpah is more than just opinionated. Anyone can have an opinion, and more than likely it stinks. True chutzpah contains both candor and humor. It's willing to play the part of offense and defense and even throw a Hail Moses pass when necessary.

I never liked people with chutzpah. Now I realize that's because I am one.

To keep my honey-bunny (don't tell my 6'8" Norwegian giant I call him that in public) falling in love with me again and again, I get spunky with him almost daily. We partake in these informal matches of verbal haranguing. Over the last few years, I've discovered that the goal for him is not to win as much as to keep the match going as long as possible.

I throw my scrappy self into the battle and hold on for as long as possible.

These verbal matches can begin anytime, anywhere, over anything. Just yesterday one began over a magazine subscription to *Popular Mechanics* that had expired. He complained that I had asked him not to buy the subscription until some of our other magazine subscriptions ran out, since we have more than twenty. Hearing his concern, I suggested that if it was that important to him, go ahead and buy it.

He gave me a hard time about the magazine, and the match was on! It lasted for close to ten minutes, bouncing back and forth with different arguments and answers that crossed over the border into ridiculouslandia. At one point, I argued that if he didn't have so many magazines he wouldn't spend as much time in the bathroom. He answered that without magazines he would spend even more. Though the arguments were nonsensical, the banter progressed as we each deflected and distracted with our responses. We contested and contended, we declared and defended. The match finally ended when I threw my hands up in the air and said, "I won!"

Leif grabbed me, hugged me, and kissed me, and said, "No, you didn't win that one."

But I did. I won his heart again.

It's taken me a few years, but I recently figured out how to take my husband's love of verbal wrangling and use it to bring us closer together spiritually. It began with the book *The Burning Word* by Judith M. Kunst, which introduced me to a practice my Jewish grandmother had failed to mention: midrash. This rich tradition invites deeper exploration—including study, reflection, and debate—of the Scripture. Kunst describes:

> Midrash reads the Hebrew Bible not for what is familiar but for what is unfamiliar, not for what's clear but for what's unclear, and then wrestles with the text, passionately, playfully, and reverently. Midrash views the Bible as one side of a conversation, started by God, containing an implicit invitation, even command, to keep the conversation —argument, story, poem—going.

In Hebrew, Midrash means *to search out*. Midrash asks the reader to find those quirky, oddball Scriptures and inconsistencies and try to make sense of them before God. It challenges us to explore that which we do not know in order to better understand the One we want to know.

Midrash invites us to have a little chutzpah with the Bible. Like a good verbal exchange with my husband, Jewish midrash urges us to take hold of a passage, wrestle with it, and not let go until we're worn out and forcibly must cry *uncle*. Midrash has become one of the beautiful connecting points where my Jewish heritage and Christian beliefs intersect. Through this ancient practice of biblical study, I am invited into the depth of Scripture — to trade in a surface understanding for a deeper grasp of a passage's meaning. Sometimes when I finish midrash, I discover that I know less than I thought I did, but even in that, I actually know more than I did when I started.

I knew my honey-bunny would like Jewish midrash as much if not more than me. Passing along *The Burning Word* was like giving him the golden ticket to the land of biblical debate. On one Sunday morning before church, I asked him if he wanted to study the Bible together — midrash style.

He jumped at the opportunity. We began in Genesis 19, since that's where I had left off in an earlier reading, and we took a hard look at the doom of Sodom. We read of the angels entering the city, wondering what angels might be in our city at the moment. We reflected on the unthinkable act of Lot offering his own daughters to sexual predators. We read of Lot's wife, whose regretful glance cost her everything. The chapter was packed with paradoxes, ironies, and countless unanswered questions. With so many passageways to explore, we didn't know which to choose. Somehow, one chose us. We began to look at what other Scriptures said about Sodom. While passages such as the seventh verse of Jude highlight the city's reputation for sexual immorality and perversion, we stumbled on this gem in Ezekiel 16:49–50:

> "Now this was the sin of your sister Sodom: She and her daughters were arrogant, overfed and unconcerned; they

did not help the poor and needy. They were haughty and did detestable things before me. Therefore I did away with them as you have seen."

We sat in awe of this passage. Sodom is synonymous with sexual sin. Every message, illustration, or reference I heard while growing up made it clear that the twin cities of Sodom and Gomorrah were destroyed because of sodomy. More than one spiritual leader had used the Genesis account as a hallmark against sexual sin. But it's no accident that Ezekiel highlights the lack of care for the poor before he ever mentions any sexual activities. The passage uncovered something deeper for me and my husband that Sunday morning—the sexual acts were merely outward behaviors of inward attitudes. The heart issues ran deeper: the people had become prideful, self-satisfied, and apathetic.

Before this morning of midrash, I could have read Genesis 19 as a distant story in a faraway land. Now I was confronted with myself in the story.

> Arrogant. Check.
> Overfed. Check.
> Unconcerned. Check.

I am no different than anyone found in the twin sin cities. As a contributing member of an arrogant culture, whose pride reaches international proportions, I make my donations in small ways every day—through self-righteous and better-than-you attitudes, insensitive self-serving opinions, and nationalistic tendencies and beliefs. My pride puts itself on display in the ways I shop, dress, eat, and talk, and is only compounded by the fact that I live in an overfed, prosperous society. While thousands are quietly starving, I'm busy buying a twelve-pack of paper towels at Costco. Such bounty reveals that real poverty comes from both lack of access as well as abundance of excess. The result is an unconcerned, apathetic response to those in need which almost reads like an equation:

Arrogant + Overfed = Unconcerned

Now, that doesn't mean I'm not quick to respond to need —especially my own—but when it doesn't concern me, involve me, or somehow help me, there's a tendency to get only minimally involved or worse, not get involved at all.

That may sound cold and naked, but that's how the passage in Ezekiel made me feel. I quietly asked the Organic God to do something and anything in me at the same time. The desire became a two-word prayer: *Change me.*

Leif eventually closed out our time of midrash study and we went to church. But I couldn't shake eight words from the Ezekiel passage: *They did not help the poor and needy.*

I thought about going to the grocery store and buying items

for a local food bank, but the afternoon filled up with activities and I never got around to going shopping.

The next morning I went to buy a parking pass at the airport for an upcoming trip. On a whim, the woman gave me the pass for free. It was the equivalent of handing me more than fifty dollars in cash. I smiled, thanked the gracious woman, and left feeling grateful and humble. All I could think was, *How many gifts can I possibly contain before I begin to give back?*

I couldn't stand it anymore. That was my tipping point — the moment when I knew something had to give and that something was me.

I drove straight to the grocery store, and with a mad dash that resembled *Supermarket Sweep*, began filling up the cart with products for the local food bank. I piled the cart with dozens of items and entered the checkout lane with a full basket and more importantly an overflowing heart. I delivered the food that afternoon and for the first time in two days felt a sense of peace.

Through that experience, which began with midrash, something very personal came together for me. I felt as if God was giving me a strategy on how to survive when you find yourself living in and succumbing to an arrogant, overfed, unconcerned society: Care for those who have less than you.

Have you ever noticed that when God really wants to get your attention, he says the same thing in countless different ways? Genesis 19 is only one of the ways God has been whispering his concern for the poor into my life. I see it time and time again — through movies, videos, magazine articles, newspaper clippings, Scriptures, conversations, sermons, and friends. The message is being scrawled on the walls of my life. Serve the poor and needy. Give voice to those who cannot speak for themselves. Protect the defenseless.

God is unbelievably stubborn in his concern for us. He does not give up. He does not give in. Indeed, God is very stubborn. If seen in a negative light, stubbornness is often synonymous with being inflexible and bullheaded. But God's unwillingness to yield — his stubbornness, if you will — is not haphazard. It's founded in his love — his firmly resolved, absolutely determined, unrelenting love.

Consider a moment of midrash on the actual words of Jesus. I have read the Sermon on the Mount so many times that it has become a mainstay of my spiritual diet. As I read and reread the rich red words, I marvel that in just a few pages, Jesus drew a stunning picture of life in his kingdom.

I recently read Jesus's sermon from the perspective of what it really said about God. What could I uncover about him? Often when I read the Sermon on the Mount, I pick out the various jewels tucked within the text. I read the Beatitudes or the Lord's Prayer or the story of the wise man who built his house on the rock, and I find individually applicable insights and truths in each one.

I just finished reading Jesus's sermon from a different perspective: I read it from the understanding that everything in the teaching is pushing us toward a relationship with God. Jesus is introducing his Father and the Holy Spirit and inviting us into a living relationship with him. He is peeling back the layers of rules for human religious behavior and inviting us to interact with the living God.

Jesus launches us into this mind-set by turning the logic of the listeners on its head. He offers blessing to the poor in spirit, those who mourn, the gentle, the merciful, the peacemakers, and those who are persecuted for doing God's good work. In God's economy, those who are humble, merciful, pure, and peaceful are the richest of all. Jesus then proceeds to reveal our true identity as children of God. As his kids, we are naturally different. We don't blend in. We are like the basic elements of salt and light, substances that naturally change and influence everything they contact. We are to flavor and illuminate the world around us to the glory of God.

Our personal relationships are even affected by our connection with God. Jesus speaks of forgiveness, reconciliation, and holiness. He goes so far as to raise the bar on some of the Ten Commandments. Don't murder, in fact, don't even call your brother a fool. Don't commit adultery, in fact, don't even look on another with lust. Even the standards on broken marriages and oaths are raised a notch. The idea of an eye for an eye and a tooth for a tooth is replaced with the law of love.

As if challenging the way we interact with each other was not enough, Jesus goes one step further: he confronts the religious practices of the day. He invites his listeners to take their alms, prayers, and fasting into a secret place where no one but God will see. Then he walks into the secret places of our hearts where the worry, anxiety, and desire for money rest, and he invites us to bring them before God. In all of this, Jesus challenges us not to judge but to pray and pursue God above all else. Jesus closes by acknowledging that storms will come in life, but those who listen to and obey these teachings will find themselves on an unshakable foundation.

Jesus's sermon is brilliant. Not just because it is Jesus or because it is printed in red, but because it cuts to the core of life. His words are as relevant today as they were a few thousand years ago on a dusty, rocky mountainside. At the nucleus of his sermon, Jesus invites us into a relationship with the Organic God. He makes it clear that he is not trying to erase the law, but fulfill it, and in the process the new law becomes harder than the old, because you cannot cling to a list of dos and don'ts. Instead, the only thing to hold on to is God.

Jesus calls us to the impossible.

He doesn't just challenge our actions, but our attitudes and the very nature of our being—the stuff that only God can transform and redeem. He calls us to the place where we are unable to change on our own. At that place, he introduces God.

Simply functioning, as the Sermon on the Mount instructs, is impossible apart from God. Our ability to live as children of God is not dependent on us as much as it is on him. And he promises that he'll back us up the whole way. His commitment to us—his very stubbornness—becomes the bedrock of our faith journey. He promises to not just go before us, but with us and after us. God's presence does not negate our responsibility to know and respond to him, but everything about Jesus's sermon invites us into a deeper relationship with God.

Consider Jesus's instructions on prayer:

> "But when you pray, go into your room, close the door and pray to your Father, who is unseen. Then your Father, who sees what is done in secret, will reward you. And when you pray, do not keep on babbling like pagans, for they think they will be heard because of their many words."
>
> MATTHEW 6:6–7

Jesus invites us into a private meeting room with God—right in our homes. He encourages us to communicate with God from the heart, not just using stale, memorized prayers or poems, but those which capture our desires and imaginations and make us do seemingly crazed things. Jesus pushes us toward intimacy with God. That intimacy extends beyond our religious practices and infects our relationships with others. The very thing that Jesus commands that we do—live a life without retaliation—is impossible without God. To be the one who forgives, blesses, lets go, and moves on, invites us into maturity with God and with others.

If that is not enough, Jesus asks us to unpack our bags and live a life without worry, anxiety, and excess concern. He reminds us that the God who feeds the birds and decorates the fields knows our needs even before we recognize them ourselves. Stripped of such everyday concerns, Jesus asks us to realign our heart's focus and to continually seek God's authority as well as his righteousness in our lives. In return, we are granted a simple but powerful promise that everything else will be taken care of by God himself.

I'm thankful for a God who is both unbelievably stubborn and amazingly persistent and who keeps drawing my heart toward the things that are on his heart. I sometimes wonder how many rabbis would be willing to say that God has chutzpah. Even if he doesn't, I'm glad that he allows us to have some chutzpah with one another—and with his Word.

I wonder what the next morning of midrash will bring.

.009 Abundantly Kind

WHILE ADJUSTING TO MARRIED LIFE WITH LEIF HAS BEEN relatively smooth and easy, adjusting to life in Alaska has been one of the most difficult things I have ever done. In addition to the more than three hundred days of rain a year, the dark, soggy winters have taken a toll on my spirit.

When I first moved here, older, wiser women would gently put their arms around me and say, "It gets better." I had no idea what they were talking about. How could this mold-infested downpour of a life possibly get better?

With each winter, I have discovered the truth neatly tucked within their kind words. It really does get better. You slowly learn what it takes to survive. You travel. You keep busy. You buy a Happy Light. You get a prescription for antidepressants. I have tried all of those things at one time or another and all of them at once, but with each passing winter they become less necessary.

This past winter, a friend remarked how frustrated she had been with the rain—it had been pouring for sixteen days in a row. I hadn't even noticed. Putting my arm around her, I offered a promise I knew to be true: "It gets better."

Though I've learned how to survive the long winters and rainy climate, I still struggle with some of the challenges that accompany life in a pioneering state. From the limited shopping to the lack of familiar cultural activities, an unmistakable sense of separation, and at times, isolation, comes with living in Alaska.

The state is part of America and yet geographically it's far removed from the other states. I'm reminded of this every time I step on a plane. The long days of traveling, particularly when it's work related, are exhausting. From time to time, travelers get rather testy. Just recently I was on an Alaska Airline flight from Juneau, Alaska, to Seattle, Washington, when I noticed a woman brave enough to put her seat all the way back. It turned out to be a rather unpopular move. Halfway through the flight, the man behind her needed to get up to use the restroom, but he couldn't get out of his seat because of the woman's weight on her seat back. Angry and frustrated, he told her, "I can't get out of my seat. Could you finally put your seat up?" She was startled by his gruff voice and quickly responded by pushing the silver button on her armrest. The man made a beeline toward the restroom. As he returned to his seat, he refused to make eye contact with her.

When the flight landed, the man was still avoiding any interaction with the woman, so she made the first move.

"I am so sorry about the seat. I had no idea it was back that far. Will you please forgive me?" she asked.

The man was clearly humbled by the sweet tone and kind words of the woman. "I shouldn't have been so obnoxious about it," he apologized. He quickly distracted himself by looking for his bag in the overhead bin, but she graciously persisted in the apology. The man clearly became uncomfortable and embarrassed by the kindness. The transformation could be seen in him and felt within the atmosphere of the cabin.

Kindness contains an unmistakable transforming power, not just when you're on long flights in Alaska. Kindness is disarming—especially when delivered in unexpected moments. Kindness has the ability to change our attitudes and responses, transforming the way we interact with others and the world. Even hardened hearts melt in the presence of kindness. Something about the nature of kindness pierces the soul, accentuating our own humanity and reminding us that we, too, can be kind.

In the search to know the Organic God, I have been surprised to discover that he is abundantly kind. Sure, I was familiar with his love and his grace, but his kindness caught me unaware. Now it's hard for me to read more than a portion of Scripture without encountering his abundant kindness.

God's kindness reached down from heaven in the person of Jesus Christ. One of the key motivations behind this extravagant grace was kindness. God saw humanity beyond redemption and sent a redeemer. It wasn't deserved or the fulfillment of an IOU—but an act of love which manifested itself in kindness, an expression of covenantal love—a willingness to honor the commitment to love, even when treated badly. Titus 3:4–5 acknowledges, "But when the kindness and love of God our Savior appeared, he saved us, not because of righteous things we had done, but because of his mercy."

The riches of God, including his kindness, are like a never-ending story. They flow from within the very nature of God, a manifestation of his holy love and goodness toward creation. I cannot get to know God apart from his kindness. If I am to know God as he really is, then I must not just accept that God is kind, I must embrace his kindness as my own. I need that kindness to saturate my being and transform me.

Awhile back, I found myself living life in overdrive—the kind of busy where you're burning the candle on both ends as well as in the middle. Completely maxed out, I was living at a speed and capacity greater than my life could contain. My relationship with God suffered. Actually, it wasn't just my relationship with God, it was every relationship, but in his kindness, he was the first to speak up.

Tired of living on peanut butter, crackers, and canned corn, I took time out of an already busy schedule to buy fresh provisions. I carefully calculated the shortest checkout line at the store, completed my purchase, and rushed to the car. While transferring the groceries from the cart to the car, a crystal-clear thought overwhelmed my mind: *I miss you.*

The voice was so loud that it could have been audible, but it was not. There was no one around. I instantly knew the voice. God had spoken. No question. No doubt. Just a sudden sense of remorse. How could I have gotten so busy as to ignore the One who desires a relationship with me above all else?

My eyes welled up and my soul softened as I prayed a quiet but heartfelt, *I'm sorry, and I miss you too.* The experience was one of the most tender interactions with God I have ever had. I was deeply moved and still am to this day, not because God's words made me feel shame or guilt, but because they were bathed in his kindness. I don't know if God could have spoken any kinder words to me at the time. His kindness was an invitation to come back into relationship with him, and I couldn't help but respond.

God's kindness also reminded me that he favors the weak, and his invitation to rest is extended to the most tired of souls. Jesus describes his yoke as "easy," not because he demands less of us, but because he bears more of the weight himself. The yoke of Jesus is lined with kindness, and obeying God's laws brings restoration to our souls.

Such abundant kindness is overwhelming. How can someone who has so much, grace someone who has so little? Why does God choose to be kind to me?

This manifestation of God's grace cannot be explained; all I know is that I hunger for his kindness. Something in the depths of my being longs for it. The more I encounter kindness, the more I can show kindness to others.

Looking back, I realize that I was affected by the woman who extended kindness on that Alaska Airlines flight. Interestingly, that same day I had the opportunity to offer it as well. On a later flight, which was quite full, I noticed that the way the seats were configured, the man to the right of me had taken my under-the-seat storage space for his own. The overhead bins were completely packed without room for another bag. A stewardess standing nearby noticed the predicament and asked the man to move his brown leather bag. He refused. In a stern voice, he announced he was not going to move his things.

I offered to have my carry-on checked, but the stewardess continued citing airline policy. He eventually caved. I watched as he followed the same behavior as the gruff man from the previous flight. He avoided any possible eye contact with me and seemed stoic. The two people beside me undoubtedly felt the tension in the air. I decided to follow the example of the woman I had watched the day before. I gently tapped the man on the shoulder and apologized for the packed airline cabin and lack of room for carry-ons. I knew it wasn't my fault the flight was full, but I also knew that a kind tone would go a long way. The man immediately apologized and explained the long, difficult, and tiring journey he had been on. For more than twenty minutes, he went on to share stories of living in Alaska. The remainder of the flight was comfortable and peaceful. On the way off the plane, he even helped me with my bag—a reminder that kindness truly is contagious.

Kindness is largely learned, and God often chooses to display his kindness through people. Throughout my life, I have met countless people who have taught me mini lessons of kindness. Teachers who were patient with me in those moments when I didn't catch on to a new lesson quickly. Friends who graciously forgave me for some awful behavior, and in the process taught me how to forgive. Strangers who extended hospitality to me when I was traveling through a foreign land. All kinds of people have taught me what it means to be kind.

When we grow close to God and when we hunger after him, we can't help but encounter his kindness, and it sprouts inside of us like fruit. That kindness invites us to recognize the needs of others and take the steps necessary to meet those needs. Not all our acts of kindness will be heroic. We will never be able to meet all the needs, answer all the questions, or perform all kinds of extraordinary feats, but we can choose kindness so that it becomes an extension of who we are in all that we do.

During a recent surgery, I discovered what a tremendous difference kindness can make. I entered the short-term day-surgery ward of the local hospital and was greeted by an extremely kind and thoughtful nurse who went out of her way to make me feel comfortable. She was informative and made me feel instantly at ease. This nurse made my stay pleasant with her warm blankets and generous efforts to make me as cozy as possible as we waited for an opening in the operating room.

I awoke from surgery to a very different nurse. This person was so loud and gruff that I felt like I was being yelled at. In a loud voice, she asked, "Do you know where you are?" and bombarded me with several questions at once. The harshness of her voice made me shut down rather than want to wake up. All I could think was that I just wanted her to stop yelling at me. Why wouldn't she take my hand and speak to me nicely? Why wouldn't she be soothing and kind—especially after I had come through something as traumatic as having an organ removed from my body?

I curled toward the side I had been operated on in my limited efforts to get away from the nurse. I didn't speak. I had only one thought running through my head, *I am a person, not a product, please treat me like a person.* I don't know how long I was in the recovery room, but I finally remember getting enough wits about me to ask to be returned to the nice nurse and my husband. I literally begged, "Please, please take me back." I was finally taken back to the short-term day-surgery ward, where I was reassured by the kind nurse.

I still don't know what happened to the gruff nurse. Maybe she was having a bad day. Maybe she had never been in a situation where she needed someone to speak to her kindly. But I learned a valuable lesson in just what a tremendous difference kindness can make, particularly when you are in a vulnerable situation.

As part of humanity, we are all in a vulnerable situation. We are susceptible to disappointments, disease, pain, and all the things that come with living in an imperfect world. That is why kindness — particularly God's kindness — is so important. Simple acts of kindness put us at ease. They impart hope. At times, they make all the difference.

Occasionally, a display of kindness may have no visible effect. The person may keep the same tone or walk away with the same outward demeanor, but something still changes in us when we allow kindness to win out in the battle of our hearts. Like the redemption scene from one of my all-time favorite holiday cartoons *The Grinch Who Stole Christmas*, kindness makes our hearts grow larger. When we pour our energy into someone else — whether it's saving a sleigh full of gifts or simply extending kindness to a stranger — we discover new reserves of strength. Like the Grinch, our hearts can grow three sizes in a single day.

Kindness doesn't usually make such grand displays except in holiday cartoons. Instead, kindness makes itself real in the smallest of actions. A gentle smile. A listening ear. A warm reply. A door held open for a stranger. Kindness means doing someone else's chores, filling a stranger's gas tank, or running an errand for a neighbor. Such simple, everyday activities put kindness on display for the world to see, and they reveal hidden strength.

That's why it should be no wonder kindness is attractive; it has a magnetic quality. Jeremiah 31:3 says, "The LORD appeared to us in the past, saying: 'I have loved you with an everlasting love; I have drawn you with loving-kindness.'" God's kindness is part of a committed promise — his covenantal love — to us. This love tugs at our heartstrings and serves as an invitation to come into a closer relationship with him.

Tucked into the Old Testament is a rather extraordinary story of kindness. King David of Israel was a man who lived hungry after God. Despite wrinkles in his character, including an affair with Bathsheba, not to mention the murder of her husband, God pursued David throughout his life. When he became king, David remembered the promises he had made to the households of Jonathan and Saul, and he went out of his way to find someone from their bloodline to whom he could show kindness.

Second Samuel 9:1–3 introduces the story:

> David asked, "Is there anyone still left of the house of Saul to whom I can show kindness for Jonathan's sake?" Now there was a servant of Saul's household named Ziba. They called him to appear before David, and the king said to him, "Are you Ziba?" "Your servant," he replied. The king asked, "Is there no one still left of the house of Saul to whom I can show God's kindness?" Ziba answered the king, "There is still a son of Jonathan; he is crippled in both feet."

Ziba suggests a below-the-radar-screen candidate: Mephibosheth. Dropped by his nurse when he was only five years old, Mephibosheth was a cripple on the run. Afraid that he would be killed by the new king, he took refuge in a barren place called Lo Debar, meaning "no pasture."

At first, the kindness is born out of a sense of obligation. David is showing kindness *for Jonathan's sake.* But when David interacts with Ziba, the focus becomes revealing God's kindness. God takes center stage in the story, and we read that any kindness shown by David is really a reflection of the covenantal promise. Often, we emphasize kindness as a spontaneous action, but biblical kindness operates on the basis of covenantal love. It parallels the story of our own redemption.

David found Mephibosheth in the barren land and brought him back to his kingdom and invited him to eat at the king's table. Jesus in his great kindness searches for us in the barren land of life and invites us to feast with God at the great wedding feast of the Lamb. This story offers a reflection of God's generous invitation through Jesus. Just as David reached out to Mephibosheth in the brokenness of humanity, God reaches out to us in our own brokenness.

It is one thing to extend kindness to those who don't deserve it, but it is another thing to extend kindness to those who are ungrateful or unkind. Luke 6:35–36 says, "But love your enemies, do good to them, and lend to them without expecting to get anything back. Then your reward will be great, and you will be sons of the Most High, because he is kind to the ungrateful and wicked. Be merciful, just as your Father is merciful."

Yet this is the point where things get shaky for me. To express kindness to those who are unappreciative, difficult to be around, or downright obnoxious — that's when I'm forced to reflect on just how kind or unkind I really am.

We live in Juneau, and in addition to living in the state capital, we have another advantage: we have Costco. It's the smallest Costco store in the country. We don't even have rotisserie chickens. But for those who live in southeastern Alaska, visiting Juneau is an opportunity to come to the big city and shop. As a result, we have lots of houseguests.

Most of the people who stay with us are gracious and kind. We open up our home and lives and thoroughly enjoy the warm meals and time together. But I recently had a guest who challenged my ability to be kind. The guest had stayed with us for several days on different occasions and took full advantage of anything we offered, but without any sense of appreciation. Instead, I felt from them a sense of entitlement to kindness, and in the end, I felt used. My kindness toward this person was all used up. I was running on empty.

On the inside I was having a debate. On one hand, I don't believe in being taken advantage of or being a doormat. This guest had other places to stay in the area, and didn't need to stay at our home. On the other hand, I want to be kind, regardless of appreciation.

When I read the command to "love your enemies, do good to them, and lend to them without expecting to get anything back," a bucket of cold water is splashed across my face. The command to love, do good, lend, and be kind does not discriminate but is extended to everyone — even unappreciative houseguests. Clearly, the first half of the verse focuses on our actions, but the latter half is really about attitude and expectations.

The hard truth is that when I show kindness, I expect something in return. Sometimes that expectation is a sense of satisfaction, a smile on a person's face, or a word of thanks. I can try to pretend that expectation isn't there, but time and time again, I see the desire resurface. I can't deny its presence, but I can make sure it doesn't get the best of me.

The times in life when I get the most hurt in relationships, the moments when I am most tempted to pull back, are when my expectations are out of line. When I expect someone to respond in one way and they choose another, I get disappointed or hurt. In this verse in Luke, Jesus offers a word of wisdom and encouragement: drop your expectations. I have interpreted this in my own life to mean that people cannot give you what they do not have. In other words, if the houseguest who stayed with us really had the grace to say "thank you," reciprocate, or even buy a card, the guest would have done it. The person did not. Maybe they don't travel much or have not had very many guests or have not realized the fullness of God's kindness. Whatever the reason, when I realize that they did not give what they did not have, I am set free. In my heart, I can be kind again.

A renewal or restoration takes place when I give up the sense that I am owed something. I am able to give freely, not expecting anything in return. I can put aside the fear of exploitation.

This idea of extending kindness is tested again and again for me. Sometimes I fare better than others. The more I experience God's abundant kindness, the more I fall in love with him and naturally want to express that love to others, regardless of the response—and the more I find myself content right where I am—even in Alaska. In fact, I find this place molding me into a kinder person, someone who is discovering rich reservoirs of patience and learning how to forgive. The rain. The climate. The isolation. Alaska isn't an easy place to live, but that's part of the state's intrigue and what makes it unique. You don't shape the land here as much as it shapes you. And with God's grace, I find myself becoming a little more pliable, more relaxed, and—dare I say it—even more mature with each passing winter. Through the dark months, I get more than a handful of opportunities to practice patience and forgiveness —just as others get to practice them with me. As a result, I've seen my attitude change toward Alaska, not as a place we have to be (for my husband's work), but one that we get to be—a place of personal growth and wild beauty. In God's abundant kindness, he has placed us here. And I am grateful.

.010 Deeply Mysterious

WHILE WINTERS IN ALASKA ARE HARSH, THEY ARE NO comparison to the brilliance of the summers. This is the land where icy deep-blue waters greet steep, green rugged mountains, which meet white snow-capped mountain peaks. The natural scenes are beauty unimaginable. Regal bald eagles and black ravens fill the air while a variety of whales, salmon, and otters dance in the waters below. On a sunny day, Alaska is one of the most spectacular places in the world.

Whether you've lived here for several years or a lifetime, an unmistakable thrill accompanies an encounter with the animals that reside here—especially the bears. Their strength, power, smell, and scat are unforgettable. In the spring and fall, they lose their shyness and invade our streets, yards, and trashcans. During these times of the year, smart pet owners know better than to leave Fido out on a leash unless they want their furry friend to become a bear snack. I have had run-ins with bears while hiking as well as on the way to the grocery store, post office, and Blockbuster. Grizzlies and black bears can be seen roaming through a neighbor's yard or an empty field, or sometimes crossing the street. The encounters are terrifying and tantalizing all at the same time.

Living in Alaska is a lot like living in a zoo, but the animals are the ones who roam free. At night, the humans are locked in their homes in order to keep safe.

While bears and eagles and sea lions still leave me in awe, the glaciers repeatedly take my breath away. The very first time I encountered a glacier was here in Juneau. I had seen a volcano bubbling with lava, coral reefs teeming with rainbow-colored fish, as well as Old Faithful and the Grand Tetons. I thought a visit to Mendenhall Glacier would be a nice outing in the been-there-done-that-check-it-off-the-list kind of way. I didn't expect the encounter to render me speechless. As we came down the road toward the glacier, I was awed by its beauty and power.

The enormous glacier stretched into the mountains as far as the eye could see. The icy surface wasn't easily contained. Filling the entire valley like a down comforter, the glacier was anything but soft, warm, or safe. The frozen surface was scarred by deep crevasses. Along the rough exterior, rocks as small as pebbles and as large as elephantine boulders stained the snowy surface. The glacier was on the move, and it was changing everything it touched.

In its wake, the glacier was transforming the land. The valley took on a new design that was wider, and in some areas, smoother. Many of the rocks that the glacier touched became nothing more than fine silt, a kind of glacier tell that feels like powder to the touch. Even the vegetation that springs up in the wake of the glacier was different—more tender and rich with a vibrant youthful green.

Since that initial encounter, the glacier has become a kind of personal holy place where I go to reflect on the attributes of the Organic God.

The glacier makes me think of God, because like God, it is big, powerful, and constantly on the move. I have spent afternoons on the silt-filled banks of the lake at the foot of the icy mass. For hours on end, nothing appears to be happening. Ever so slowly, its presence is moving, carving, purifying, and reshaping everything with which it comes into contact.

In some ways this reminds me of my faith: those moments when I cry out in prayer asking God to act or respond. Too often, it doesn't look or feel like he's doing anything, but like the glacier, he is on the move.

One of the places in my life where this simple but transforming truth is most real to me is in a Bible study group I regularly attend. Some time ago, I was in a place where I knew I needed to have people actively praying for me. I explained the situation to my associate pastor, who immediately knew where to send me: the Wednesday morning Christ Care group. I was greeted by more than a dozen women from all walks of life. Their warm smiles, humor, and honesty were contagious, and I immediately found myself feeling at home among these Alaskan women, all of whom were three to four decades older than me.

Since joining, I have learned everything I didn't want to know about hot flashes and menopause. I've discovered secrets of the golden years, some of which are not that golden, as the challenges that accompany retirement and deteriorating health abound.

Among this group, I have also been able to watch the lives of these women, these saints, many of whom have been followers of Jesus, discovering the Organic God throughout their entire lives. They know him and are known by him. They have been marked by his presence. The words they speak, their attitudes, and their actions testify that God has been active in their lives.

We study. We talk. We pray. I'm both amazed and humbled to watch week-in and week-out as God answers specific prayers of all sizes, shapes, and levels of urgency. Together we have prayed for people facing death, disease, decision, transition, and opportunity. We have prayed for the young and the old, the rich and the poor, and even a few pets along the way.

God rest Fido's soul.

The Lord doesn't just hear our prayers. He answers — though

not always with the answer that we want or hope. Yet there's little doubt that he is involved.

One of the women shared a tender story of God being fully alive in her life that still haunts me. She and her husband have been struggling with one of their adult sons for years. The relationship has been strained at best, and poor decisions on the son's part have compounded an already difficult situation. As a mom, she has prayed countless prayers asking God to heal and restore. The son still chooses to go his own way.

One day, this woman found herself overwhelmed and desperate. She had reached the end of herself—feelings of loss and disappointment stained her soul. She cried out to God, *Are you going to save my son? Are you even listening?* At that moment, she felt God whisper two simple but powerful words to her: *I am.*

Two words. Three letters. The exact words this aching mom says she needed to hear. In two syllables God let her know that he was still in control, he had heard her prayers, and he had not left the scene. Nothing had escaped his notice. He was still as active and involved as ever. God was fully alive in the situation.

I am.

Listening to this story, my hunger for the Organic God comes alive again. Like the glacier, even when I don't think anything is happening, his powerful presence is still in motion. God is still on the move. I want his reality, the God-reality, to permeate my life so that I don't just know that God is fully alive but that his presence becomes transformational within me.

I am doing.

I am alive.

I am here.

I am.

When I see God's name mentioned in Scripture, I often find a verb somewhere nearby. God is constantly on the move. Though we may not always see him or sense him, he is actively engaged.

Consider for a moment a few of the verbs of God.

God answers, bestows, blesses, blots, calls, cares, cleanses, clothes, comforts, corrects, counsels, covers, cuts off, delights, delivers, detests, disciplines, encourages, fills, forgives, gathers, gives, guards, guides, heals, hears, helps, holds, increases, keeps, knows, leads, lifts, listens, loves, opens, pours, preserves, protects, provides, purifies, rejoices, remembers, rescues, restores, rewards, satisfies, saves, speaks, strengthens, sustains, teaches, upholds, watches, works, and wounds.

Indeed, our God is fully alive. He is ever-present. He is ever-active. He is ever-involved.

No matter what my emotions or mind or circumstances may try to tell me, the truth is that God is not only present, he has movement. God is not a spectator; he is actively engaged. He is on the move.

God's presence in my life is like the glacier in that he is constantly pressing down, re-landscaping, and renovating the very core of who I am. He is breaking up the boulders and smoothing out the rockiest parts of my soul. He is reshaping me, and in the process he is redeeming. Like the glacier, God leaves a trail of new life behind him.

Recently, I found myself enjoying a thrilling afternoon with friends in a water park. We raced down Splashdown, swam in Commotion Ocean, and floated down Castaway Creek. Leif decided he wanted to try the Acapulco Cliff Dive, a sixty-five-foot-tall high-speed free-fall slide. Knowing what the ride would inadvertently do to my swimsuit, I decided to hang out at the bottom of the slide and watch.

That's when I saw him.

He was only five years old. A purplish-blue birthmark stained the right side of his face, his neck, his arm — all the way down to his fingers. I couldn't take my eyes off the unruly discoloration or the boy who was smiling wildly, sparkling with glee. He was ready for another round in the wave pool.

I stared at that dark blemish, knowing the social pain waiting the boy as he grew older, and a single question sprang from my heart, *Why, God?*

I solemnly offered those two words in what sounded more like a pang than a prayer. The question I was asking God was about so much more than the boy. Why, God, do we live in a fallen world? Why, God, do we live with so much suffering? Why, God, do we live with so much imperfection?

One soul-piercing sentence flooded my mind: *You don't know the plans I have for him.* I breathed deeply, releasing the tension I felt in my soul. I recognized my pride in assuming that I knew what was best for this young boy, my pride in assuming that that blemish had escaped God's notice, my pride in assuming that somehow God couldn't handle it.

I asked for God's forgiveness. I asked for his grace. I asked for a special blessing on the child.

Like the glacier, God re-landscapes my attitudes and knowledge of him. In unexpected places, God continues the transformation and purification process.

I have been to Mendenhall Glacier many times, and even if I go two days in a row or twice in the same day, the glacier never

looks the same. The glacier always exposes something new
about itself. Sometimes the lighting makes it look different.
Sometimes a batch of new snow has fallen and painted the
surface a radiant white. Other times, the warmth of a summer's
day exposes layers deep into the glacier's being.

That's when the mysterious glacier blue appears, a type of blue
that borders on indescribable. Glacier ice is illuminated by a
luscious blue; the kind of luscious reserved for high-end lip
balm and the kind of blue that only true artists can believably
paint. Scientists give this phenomenon a rational explanation:
The red (long wavelengths) of white light is absorbed by
the ice, while the blue (short wavelengths) is scattered and
transmitted. The further the light travels, the more blue it
appears.

I have a less scientific explanation: God loves to paint the world
beautiful.

Glacial ice reflects a type of splendor and wonder and depth
that reminds me that God is big, active, powerful, and deeply
mysterious. Some things about him cannot be explained. Just
like the scientists, theologians can provide definitions and
descriptions and debate, but in the end, some things about
God are beyond explanation. They are simply mysterious.

Slowly I am discovering that the Organic God often hides
in the great big blue—in the shadows of prophecy and

unfulfilled expectation. He constantly invites us to further exploration of himself and his ways. He welcomes us into the wonder of himself: invisible and unsearchable. It's almost as if the Organic God enjoys mystery. He abides in unapproachable light. He seals and conceals knowledge. He describes himself as the beginning and the end, yet he wraps both the story of creation and the story of his final coming in mystery. He offers glimpses, insights, and clues, but still veils many of the details in a shroud of the unknown.

In the New Testament, we find a handful of spiritual mysteries, including the incarnation; the union of Christ with the church; and the resurrection of the body, among others. While *mystery* often refers to knowledge being withheld, the mystery described in the New Testament refers to knowledge that has been revealed. Yet even with such disclosures, so much about God remains unknown, and for me, that is part of the intrigue.

That's particularly true when it comes to God's redemptive purposes through Christ. He has set in motion a story of love and redemption that he alone can write and that he alone can fulfill. He alone will be acknowledged when the final credits roll. Despite being the director, producer, writer, cinematographer, star, and of course, designer of special effects, God invites us into the story—his story—and gives us a part to play that was reserved specifically for us. He invites us to take our cues from him, and in the process, enter a relationship with him and with each other like no other relationship we can ever experience — where we are both pursued and pursuer.

Why is God deeply mysterious? Why does he not just place everything on the table? In our great state of unknowing, theologians have developed a list of explanations. Some argue that our unknowing began when Adam and Eve were booted from the garden. Access to the tree of knowledge of good and evil was denied because it was more than we could bear. We can know too much for our own good. Some argue that certain secrets are to be revealed at their proper time. Even Jesus told the disciples he had more to tell them, but they could not handle it all at that moment. Others argue that our own inability to understand the truth prevents us from unveiling the mystery. Others point to the earthly limitations that come with simply being human. And still others believe that the gradual revelations of the mysteries of God are part of the divine plan. Like midrash, they give us the opportunity to embrace and grow in our faith.

As I reflect on the mysterious nature of the Organic God, I must humbly admit that I don't think I would like God very much if he wasn't mysterious. Imagine for a moment if God was finite. Imagine if he was stripped of his omnipotence and omnipresence. Imagine if God could only be in one place at a time, and like some action hero, his power supply could be cut off. I don't think I would want to serve or worship a god who could be fully understood. His mystery is part of the intrigue for me. It adds an element of luminescence.

His mystery is also part of the frustration. First Corinthians 13:12 tells us that while we now see in a mirror a poor reflection, one day we will see face-to-face. Bronze was one of the Corinthians' primary resources, and they often made their mirrors from this type of metal. The mirror referred to in this passage is most likely bronze, and the reflection in the reader's mind is given a brownish tan metallic hue—an imperfect, dim, earthy reflection—a far cry from the modern glass mirrors most of us use today. Just like the Corinthians, I, too, have a dim, earthly understanding of the world we live in.

Things don't make sense.

Things don't add up.

Things don't come together.

I find myself asking one question above all others: Why?

You've probably asked it yourself from time to time—and not just when you're at a water park. It's almost as if God in his mysterious nature, and we, in our limited perspective, are designed to circle around this question time and time again.

On a personal level one of my biggest "Why" questions has

always been: *Why did my Jewish grandmother never come to recognize Jesus as the Messiah?*

Now I know that it's impossible to know what happens to someone in the final moments before their death. I know that some people find God but never make it public. I know that she may surprise me with a bowl of matza ball soup at the pearly gates—okay, maybe not literally. I know a laundry list of pat answers that offer a sense of hope and resolve, but really, in my most honest heart of hearts, I don't have one tangible sign, expression, or hope that she ever recognized Jesus as the Messiah.

Why?

I wonder why, because I began praying for her to know Jesus when I was only five, and I kept praying for her until the day of my graduation from college when we received news of her death. I prayed thousands of prayers. I begged God. In a theologically questionable move that only a desperate seven-year-old child would make, I offered God to take my own salvation if he would just reveal himself and redeem her.

The years passed. The prayers funneled toward heaven. The opportunities to talk about my faith grew fewer and farther between. Alzheimer's, with all its cruelness, ran its course. In the end, my grandmother was reduced to a shell of a human, and as far as I know, no closer to a relationship with Jesus.

That religious tension between two worlds, between the prophesied Messiah and the Messiah fulfilled, erupted once again. I found myself asking, *Why?*

More than a decade later, I'm still asking why. That's the thing about any good *Why* question; it doesn't really go away with time. In another ten or twenty years, the question will still make me lift my brow in a failed attempt to increase the surface tension of the liquid around my eyeballs so the tears won't fall. In another decade or two or three or four, this *Why* question will still be as fresh as warm manure when I think about it.

While the names, situations, and details may differ, I think we all have our *Why* questions.

Why the abuse?
Why the injustice?
Why the suffering?
Why the silence?
Why?

Such questions are a sign that we've stepped in it — the reality that as a part of humanity, we live not just in a fallen world, but in a broken world that stinks.

The more I learn about the Organic God, the more I realize that he does not fear such questions. He does not plug his nose to the stench of humanity. He does not push back. Like an organic farmer, he is able to use the poopy parts of life as rich soil for growing the fruit of the Spirit in us.

I think God welcomes tough questions. The God who asks everything of us invites us to ask anything of him. He answers our questions with questions of his own.

Can you probe the limits of the Almighty?
Is anything too hard for me?
Can you fathom the mysteries of God?
For who has known the mind of the Lord that he may instruct him?

God's questions are far more revealing than our own. While our questions reveal our doubt, fear, and pain, his questions reveal his strength, wisdom, and power. Our questions reveal our desire to pull back. His reveal his plan to move forward. Our questions reveal our finiteness. His reveal his infinite nature. Our questions reveal our limited scope. His reveal his all-encompassing presence.

Such questions also reveal the single most mysterious thing about God: Why does an all-powerful, all-present, all-knowing God choose to use us in his redemptive plan?

This is the biggest mystery of all. In a nutshell, God sends his Son to redeem the world. The Son, after fulfilling his commission, turns around and says, "I send you!"

When we ask God our *Why* questions, he responds with a greater *Why* question:

Why not you?
Why don't you stop the abuse of others?
Why don't you fight against injustice?
Why don't you provide comfort for the suffering?
Why don't you speak up for those who cannot speak for themselves?
Why not you?

The God who does great, unsearchable, mysterious things and wonders without number invites us to be in on the action. That is the biggest mystery of all. Even though I have no answer to the question of why my Jewish grandmother never came to recognize Jesus as the Messiah, I am challenged with a simple but powerful question:

Why not you?

Just because I have no resolution on the issue of my grandmother does not mean there cannot be resolution for others—other members of my family, other friends, other neighbors, and other people. Just because my understanding of God is dim at best does not mean that God is not at work and that the invitation to join him in that work is any less real.

Maybe that's the place where my Jewish heritage and Christian heritage meet—a place of mystery. Through tension and intrigue, I am invited on a never-ending adventure to know the Organic God.

Like the glacier, my relationship with God and the *Why* questions will invariably have crevasses—deep, dark, icy pits where I can get bogged down or choose to keep moving.

When I think about people who spend more time answering the *Why* questions than asking them, I can't help but think of my friend Shane Gilbert. Outrageously talented, Shane left a successful career in Hollywood to pursue her passion of caring for the poor in Uganda. Surrounded by the countless emotional and physical scars of poverty and disease in this almost forgotten country, Shane has come to the hard, cold realization that only so much can be done with the resources they have. She works long hours in the orphanage and one day plans to make a documentary to tell the great story of Uganda.

Many of the stories Shane has shared are littered with *Why* questions. Why the abuse? Why the injustice? Why the suffering? Why the silence? Why? For some, there are enough *Why* questions to get mad at the situation and angry at God and just walk away. But Shane answers those questions day in and day out through her service at the orphanage. God's love pours through Shane to each of those children. The mysterious nature of God is manifest as she becomes the very hands and feet of Christ, and at the same time experiences his love and provision in greater measure.

Sitting at the foot of the glacier and at the feet of God, I'm in awe of what can be accomplished when even a few people choose to focus more energy on answering the *Why* questions than on asking them. In those moments, I see so many of God's attributes displayed — his bigheartedness, his amazing wisdom, his outrageous generosity, his abundant kindness, and of course, the deep mystery of how he can use people like you and me to change the world — possibly one last time.

In the cold stillness of the glacial lake, I sense God's presence, like that of a familiar old friend, and I take one step closer to the mystery that is the Organic God. As much as I have learned and discovered, there is still so far to go. If there's an ocean to travel, I'm still standing on the shore. In contemplation, I stare into the darkness, and to my amazement, I see a flicker of light as something stirs in the depth of my soul. Slowly the light begins to multiply, and I recognize that mysterious wonder of luminescence yet again.

And the hunger for God lives on.

The Organic God Soundtrack

MUSIC AWAKENS THE HEART. BELOW YOU'LL FIND A LIST
of songs to accompany your journey through this book. Be
encouraged to add a few songs of your own along the way.

.000 Luminescence

Nickel Creek, "Out of the Woods," *Nickel Creek*

Natasha Bedingfield, "Unwritten," *Unwritten*

.001 An Organic Appetite

U2, "I Still Haven't Found What I'm Looking For,"
  The Joshua Tree

Simon & Garfunkel, "Homeward Bound," *Sound of Silence*

.002 Bighearted

Norah Jones, "Come Away With Me," *Come Away With Me*

Sara Groves, "Maybe There's a Loving God," *All Right Here*

.003 Breathtakingly Beautiful

James Horner, "All Love Can Be," *A Beautiful Mind*
  Original Motion Picture Soundtrack

Mark Schultz, "Broken & Beautiful," *Broken & Beautiful*

.004 Amazingly Wise

The Fray, "How to Save a Life," *How to Save a Life*
Jared Anderson's, "Rescue," *Where to Begin*

.005 Surprisingly Talkative

Coldplay, "Talk," *X&Y*
Sarah McLachlan, "Push," *Afterglow*

.006 Wildly Infallible

James Taylor, "Fire & Rain," *Sweet Baby James*
Pearl Jam, "All Those Yesterdays," *Yield*

.007 Outrageously Generous

U2, "Grace," *All That You Can't Leave Behind*

.008 Unbelievably Stubborn

Derek Webb, "Rich Young Ruler," *Mockingbird*
Caedmon's Call, "Share the Well," *Share the Well*

.009 Abundantly Kind

Snow Patrol, "Chasing Cars," *Eyes Open*
Chris Tomlin, "Kindness," *The Noise We Make*

.010 Deeply Mysterious

Rita Springer, "You Still Have My Heart," *Rise Up*
"Holy, Holy, Holy" (any hymnal)

Behind The Scenes

.000 Luminescence

Page 08: If you don't understand what I just said, no worries, I don't
either. It took an interview with a marine biologist who has studied
bioluminescence for twenty years to concoct that sentence and
remind me that some things like falling stars and waterfalls are
better off unexplained. Special thanks to Dr. Michael Latz of the
Scripps Institution of Oceanography at the University of California,
San Diego for his insights, wit, and wisdom. Regarding the
scientific terminology, luminescence means light emission while
bioluminescence means light emission from organisms. He says that
technically the bioluminescence from South Florida is produced by
dinoflagellates, organisms that are considered protists and not plants
or animals, and "fireflies of the sea" is a term used for luminescent
ostracods, zooplankton that are a type of crustacean.

.001 An Organic Appetite

Page 16: Psalm 73:25. One of the greatest desires or hungers that I see
of men and women in both the Old and New Testaments is to know
God. Moses bravely asks God, "If you are pleased with me, teach me
your ways so I may know you and continue to find favor with you"
(Exodus 33:13). The psalmist's heart cry reverberates with a desire to
know God and his ways — "Show me your ways, O Lord, teach me
your paths; guide me in your truth and teach me, for you are God
my Savior, and my hope is in you all day long" (Psalm 25:4–5).

Page 21: If you don't have a copy of the Bible, please email me at *info@margaretfeinberg.com*, and we'll work to get you one.

Page 22: The Book of Common Prayer provides one of the best summaries of drinking from the rich wells of Scripture: "Read, mark, learn and inwardly digest."

.002 Bighearted

Page 32: I love the portrait of God dancing over us found in Zephaniah 3:17. Some translations use the phrase, "He will rejoice over you with singing," but the Hebrew meaning of the word *rejoice* means to twirl. Can you imagine God twirling in dance over you?

Page 34: I have always enjoyed independent and foreign films. I don't watch as many as I used to, but I have a long list of faves, including *Waking Ned Divine*, *The Red Balloon*, and *Hotel Rwanda*.

Page 40: Throughout Scripture, we find God's people reflecting his light to the world. I love the description found in the song and prayer of Deborah in Judges 5:31, "'So may all your enemies perish, O LORD! But *may they who love you be like the sun when it rises in its strength.*' Then the land had peace forty years" (emphasis added).

.003 Breathtakingly Beautiful

Page 53: Psalm 27:4.

Page 56: I'd really love to know your answer. Please email me at *info@margaretfeinberg.com*.

.004 Amazingly Wise

Page 59: First little known secret: I'm not very good at standardized tests. But I am good at prize drawings. I know that sounds silly, but I've won all kinds of great products, including a trip for two to Disneyland, a mountain bike, free dinners, and even a haircut.

When it comes to getting into college, I'd rather be good at standardized tests, but when it comes to life, I'd much rather be good at an old-fashioned name-in-the-hat drawing.

Second little known secret: I did have a safety school to the big four I applied to back East. It was Oral Roberts University. I thought and prayed about attending, but in the end a childhood friend who had attended the school discouraged me from going. It's amazing the role friends can have in your life.

Third little known secret: We never got our money back from that SAT prep course. After the class, the math portion of my scores tanked, but my verbal scores rose a few points. The company argued that since the verbal portion increased, they had done their job. Note to self: Always read the fine print and avoid standardized tests at all costs.

Page 69: Proverbs 2:7 NASB.

Pages 69–70: James 3:17.

Page 75: It's worth noting that of all the barn animals, this proverb chose an ox over all others—including the horse. Interestingly, other than speed, for farming the ox is superior to the horse in almost every way. Not only does an ox have a longer life and less susceptibility to disease, but it is also less expensive to feed and maintain. Ironically, the ox's manure is also more profitable (from *Adam Clarke's Commentary*, Electronic Database [Biblesoft, 1996]).

Page 76: NASB.

Page 79: Harold Myra and Marshall Shelley, *The Leadership Secrets of Billy Graham* (Grand Rapids, Mich.: Zondervan, 2005), 217.

Page 79: Mark 12:17.

Page 79: Mark 12:24–25.

Page 80: Matthew 9:12–13.

Page 80: Matthew 18:3–4.

Page 80: Maya Angelou's *I Know Why the Caged Bird Sings* is one of her most famous works.

.005 Surprisingly Talkative

Page 83: Little did I know that most of my friends were insanely jealous that I was out on the slopes with kids each day while they were making bank with 60-plus hour work weeks and major-league stress. I thought they were winning. They thought I was. It's ironic, don't ya think?

Page 87: NASB.

Page 89: Isaiah 60:16–17, emphasis added.

Page 90: Genesis 7:16.

Page 90: Exodus 11:7.

Page 96: People often ask me, "How do you know if something you heard is from God?" My response: By making lots of mistakes. Not all the nudges we feel in our innermost parts are from God. Some are from our own desires. Others from our own minds. A few can even be from the enemy. But if we never respond to any of them, we can't discover which whispers are from God and which are not. Here are seven questions I like to filter all my God-whispers through:

- Does what I heard line up with Scripture?
- Does what I heard line up with circumstance?
- Does what I heard line up with wise counsel?
- Does what I heard line up with my vision and goals?
- Does what I heard leave me with a sense of peace?
- Is this a thought I would normally think on my own?
- Is what I heard blanketed in love?

These questions have helped me tremendously in discerning God's voice in my life. For a helpful book and Bible study on hearing

God's voice, check out *The Sacred Echo: Learning to Hear God's Voice in Every Area of Your Life.*

.006 Wildly Infallible

Page 100: Growing up, my adventurous parents were never married to a particular church brand, so wherever we moved we usually attended a different denomination. As a result, during my childhood, I went to Baptist, Methodist, Episcopalian, Presbyterian, Assembly of God, as well as several non-denominational churches. When asked about my denominational background, I like to say I'm a hybrid or a mutt.

When I think of denominations today, I think of the colors of a rainbow. Some have more red and are known for their love and grace. Others are more purple and known for their prayer. Others are more green and constantly discipling and growing their members. Others are more yellow and busy highlighting causes for social justice and care for the poor. Others are more orange and known for evangelism. Each reflects a beautiful God-designed hue. Each also has its inherent strengths and weaknesses.

Page 106: Hebrews 11:1 KJV, paraphrase.

Page 108: Ephesians 2:19–22.

Page 109: Matthew 19:21–22.

.007 Outrageously Generous

Page 121: This book has been updated and rereleased as *Hungry for God: Hearing God's Voice in the Ordinary and Everyday* (Zondervan, 2011).

Page 128: John 3:16.

Page 131: See Mark 6:37.

Page 132: Deuteronomy 8:18.

Page 132: Psalm 24:1.

Page 133: Exodus 16:18.

.008 Unbelievably Stubborn

Page 140: Jews don't throw Hail Mary passes.

Page 142: Judith M. Kunst, *The Burning Word: A Christian Encounter with Jewish Midrash* (Brewster, Mass.: Paraclete, 2006), 4.

Page 143: According to Kunst, a basic Jewish midrash contains four elements. First, select a passage. Second, find a question or problem within the text. Third, use your knowledge of Scripture and your imagination to either develop an answer to the question or find something in the passage that illuminates fresh meaning in the text. Fourth, find someone to argue and explore your interpretation with. Use the Scripture as the basis for your argumentation and exploration.

.009 Abundantly Kind

Page 155: In Alaska, where I live . . .

- . . . they build large fences around the elementary schools, not so much to keep the kids in, as to keep the bears out.

- . . . we are currently experiencing around five hours of darkness a night. Only it's not really dark. It's just darker. Not quite dark enough to warrant turning on a flashlight, even at 1:00 a.m.

- . . . I have to keep an eye on our puppy, Hershey, whenever he's outside so he doesn't get taken away and eaten by an eagle.

- . . . the only chain restaurants are McDonald's and Subway.

- . . . they provide free raincoats that you can borrow when you stay at one of the local hotels.

- . . . they sell seal-skin cell phone covers.

.010 Deeply Mysterious

Page 175: God answers (Isaiah 58:9); God bestows (Proverbs 8:21); God blesses (Deuteronomy 14:29); God blots (Isaiah 43:25); God calls (1 Thessalonians 4:7); God cares (Nahum 1:7); God cleanses (Jeremiah 33:8); God clothes (Isaiah 61:10); God comforts (Isaiah 51:12); God corrects (Job 5:17); God counsels (Psalm 32:8); God covers (Psalm 91:4–6); God cuts off (John 15:1–2); God delights (Zephaniah 3:17); God delivers (Psalm 37:40); God detests (Deuteronomy 25:16); God disciplines (Proverbs 3:12); God encourages (Psalm 10:17); God fills (Job 8:21); God forgives (1 John 1:9); God gathers (Deuteronomy 30:4); God gives (Matthew 11:28); God guards (Psalm 97:10); God guides (Psalm 73:24); God heals (Hosea 14:4); God hears (Psalm 69:33); God helps (Psalm 37:40); God holds (Psalm 73:23); God increases (Deuteronomy 7:13); God keeps (Deuteronomy 7:9); God knows (Matthew 6:8); God leads (Isaiah 42:16); God lifts (Psalm 146:8); God listens (Psalm 10:17); God loves (Psalm 37:28); God opens (Deuteronomy 28:12); God pours (Isaiah 44:3); God preserves (Psalm 41:2); God protects (Psalm 41:2); God provides (Psalm 111:5); God purifies (1 John 1:9); God rejoices (Isaiah 62:5); God remembers (Psalm 111:5); God rescues (Psalm 91:14); God restores (Psalm 71:20); God rewards (Proverbs 19:17); God satisfies (Psalm 132:15); God saves (Isaiah 49:25); God speaks (Isaiah 30:21); God strengthens (Isaiah 40:29); God sustains (Psalm 55:22); God teaches (Isaiah 54:13); God upholds (Psalm 37:24); God watches (Genesis 28:15); God works (Romans 8:28); God wounds (Job 5:18). To explore the verbs of God in more depth, check out the four-session *The Verbs of God* Bible Study.

Page 178: For an explanation on glacier blue and other details on glaciology, visit *http://ak.water.usgs.gov/glaciology/FAQ.htm*.

Page 179: 1 Timothy 6:16.

Page 179: Daniel 12:9.

Page 179: 1 Timothy 3:16.

Page 179: Ephesians 5:32.

Page 179: 1 Corinthians 15:51.

Page 179: *Fausset's Bible Dictionary*, Electronic Database (Biblesoft, 1998).

Page 179: Romans 16:25; Colossians 2:2; 1 Timothy 3:9.

Page 180: John 16:12.

Page 184: "Can you probe the limits of the Almighty?" (Job 11:7); "Is anything too hard for me?" (Jeremiah 32:27); "Can you fathom the mysteries of God?" (Job 11:7); "For who has known the mind of the Lord that he may instruct him?" (1 Corinthians 2:16).

Page 185: Job 5:9.

Page 186: Shane is part of Come, Let's Dance, *www.comeletsdance.org*, a non-profit designed to help the children of Africa. Check out their websites for more information and opportunities to get involved and support their projects. Together, we can change the world.

Props

Bottomless thanks to ...

the Ferebees for undeserved support ...

Tracee Hackel for being a C. S. Lewis in my life ...

the team at Zondervan ...

my friends for listening to my wild ideas and loving me anyway ...

my husband for all those nightly prayers and morning love notes ...

the Organic God for revealing another facet of himself to me ...

Connection

Margaret Feinberg is a Bible teacher and speaker at churches and leading conferences such as Catalyst, Thrive, and Extraordinary Women. Her books and Bible studies have sold over 600,000 copies and received critical acclaim and extensive national media coverage from CNN, the Associated Press, *USA Today*, *Los Angeles Times*, *Washington Post*, and many others.

She was recently named one of 50 women most shaping culture and the church today by *Christianity Today*, one of the 30 voices who will help lead the church in the next decade by *Charisma* magazine, and one of the "40 Under 40" who will shape Christian publishing by *Christian Retailing* magazine. Margaret currently lives in Colorado with her husband, Leif and their superpup, Hershey.

One of her greatest joys is hearing from her readers. Go ahead, become her friend on Facebook, follow her on Twitter or Pinterest @mafeinberg, or check out her website.

Margaret Feinberg
Margaret@margaretfeinberg.com
www.margaretfeinberg.com
www.facebook.com/margaretfeinberg
www.twitter.com/mafeinberg

MargaretFeinberg.com

Great Resources for You, Your Book Club, and Your Small Group at www.margaretfeinberg.com.

 *Scouting the Divine* is a 6-week interactive DVD Bible study featuring 8-10 minute teaching segments that dive deep into the agrarian world of the Bible. Participants find the Bible coming alive as they learn about scripture through the eyes of a shepherd, a farmer, a beekeeper, and a vintner.

 *The Sacred Echo: Hearing God's Voice in Every Area of Your Life* 6-session DVD Bible study features 15-20 minute segments designed to help participants develop a more vibrant prayer life and recognize the repetitive nature of God's voice in their lives.

 *The Organic God* 6-session DVD Bible study featuring 8-12 minute segments looks at the attributes of God, His generosity, wisdom, bigheartedness, beauty, and more. Encounter God like you've never experienced Him before.

 *Pursuing God's Love: Stories from the Book of Genesis* reminds us of the unflinching love of our Creator. Even when we question God's love, God pursues us. This 6-session DVD Bible study features 15-20 minute segments designed to take participants through the entire book of Genesis.

 *Pursuing God's Beauty: Stories from the Gospel of John* offers portraits of salvation, redemption, and restoration. Filmed in an art studio, this 6-session DVD Bible study features 15-20 minute segments designed to take participants through the entire Gospel of John.

 *Wonderstruck: Awaken to the Nearness of God* 7-session DVD Bible study featuring 19-23 minute segments invites participants to explore the wonder of God's presence, friendship, forgiveness, and so much more. God is busting at the seams to display His power, glory, and might in your life.

To receive access to a FREE DVD sampler of Margaret Feinberg's DVD Bible Studies, email **sampler@margaretfeinberg.com**.

Share Your Thoughts

With the Author: Your comments will be forwarded to
the author when you send them to *zauthor@zondervan.com.*

With Zondervan: Submit your review of this book
by writing to *zreview@zondervan.com.*

Free Online Resources at
www.zondervan.com

Zondervan AuthorTracker: Be notified whenever your favorite
authors publish new books, go on tour, or post an update
about what's happening in their lives at www.zondervan.com/
authortracker.

Daily Bible Verses and Devotions: Enrich your life with daily
Bible verses or devotions that help you start every morning
focused on God. Visit www.zondervan.com/newsletters.

Free Email Publications: Sign up for newsletters on Christian
living, academic resources, church ministry, fiction, children's
resources, and more. Visit www.zondervan.com/newsletters.

Zondervan Bible Search: Find and compare Bible passages in
a variety of translations at www.zondervanbiblesearch.com.

Other Benefits: Register to receive online benefits like
coupons and special offers, or to participate in research.